t Introduction

CLAUSEWITZ Michael Howard
CLIMATE Mark Maslin
CLIMATE CHANGE Mark Maslin
CLINICAL PSYCHOLOGY Susan Llewelyn and Katie Aafjes-van Doorn
COGNITIVE NEUROSCIENCE Richard Passingham
THE COLD WAR Robert McMahon
COLONIAL AMERICA Alan Taylor
COLONIAL LATIN AMERICAN LITERATURE Rolena Adorno
COMBINATORICS Robin Wilson
COMEDY Matthew Bevis
COMMUNISM Leslie Holmes
COMPARATIVE LITERATURE Ben Hutchinson
COMPLEXITY John H. Holland
THE COMPUTER Darrel Ince
COMPUTER SCIENCE Subrata Dasgupta
CONCENTRATION CAMPS Dan Stone
CONFUCIANISM Daniel K. Gardner
THE CONQUISTADORS Matthew Restall and Felipe Fernández-Armesto
CONSCIENCE Paul Strohm
CONSCIOUSNESS Susan Blackmore
CONTEMPORARY ART Julian Stallabrass
CONTEMPORARY FICTION Robert Eaglestone
CONTINENTAL PHILOSOPHY Simon Critchley
COPERNICUS Owen Gingerich
CORAL REEFS Charles Sheppard
CORPORATE SOCIAL RESPONSIBILITY Jeremy Moon
CORRUPTION Leslie Holmes
COSMOLOGY Peter Coles
COUNTRY MUSIC Richard Carlin
CRIME FICTION Richard Bradford
CRIMINAL JUSTICE Julian V. Roberts
CRIMINOLOGY Tim Newburn
CRITICAL THEORY Stephen Eric Bronner
THE CRUSADES Christopher Tyerman
CRYPTOGRAPHY Fred Piper and Sean Murphy
CRYSTALLOGRAPHY A. M. Glazer
THE CULTURAL REVOLUTION Richard Curt Kraus
DADA AND SURREALISM David Hopkins
DANTE Peter Hainsworth and David Robey
DARWIN Jonathan Howard
THE DEAD SEA SCROLLS Timothy H. Lim
DECADENCE David Weir
DECOLONIZATION Dane Kennedy
DEMENTIA Kathleen Taylor
DEMOCRACY Bernard Crick
DEMOGRAPHY Sarah Harper
DEPRESSION Jan Scott and Mary Jane Tacchi
DERRIDA Simon Glendinning
DESCARTES Tom Sorell
DESERTS Nick Middleton
DESIGN John Heskett
DEVELOPMENT Ian Goldin
DEVELOPMENTAL BIOLOGY Lewis Wolpert
THE DEVIL Darren Oldridge
DIASPORA Kevin Kenny
DICTIONARIES Lynda Mugglestone
DINOSAURS David Norman
DIPLOMACY Joseph M. Siracusa
DOCUMENTARY FILM Patricia Aufderheide
DREAMING J. Allan Hobson
DRUGS Les Iversen
DRUIDS Barry Cunliffe
DYNASTY Jeroen Duindam
DYSLEXIA Margaret J. Snowling
EARLY MUSIC Thomas Forrest Kelly
THE EARTH Martin Redfern
EARTH SYSTEM SCIENCE Tim Lenton
ECONOMICS Partha Dasgupta
EDUCATION Gary Thomas
EGYPTIAN MYTH Geraldine Pinch
EIGHTEENTH-CENTURY BRITAIN Paul Langford
THE ELEMENTS Philip Ball
ÉMILE ZOLA Brian Nelson
EMOTION Dylan Evans
EMPIRE Stephen Howe
ENERGY SYSTEMS Nick Jenkins
ENGELS Terrell Carver
ENGINEERING David Blockley

THE ENGLISH LANGUAGE Simon Horobin
ENGLISH LITERATURE Jonathan Bate
THE ENLIGHTENMENT John Robertson
ENTREPRENEURSHIP Paul Westhead and Mike Wright
ENVIRONMENTAL ECONOMICS Stephen Smith
ENVIRONMENTAL ETHICS Robin Attfield
ENVIRONMENTAL LAW Elizabeth Fisher
ENVIRONMENTAL POLITICS Andrew Dobson
EPICUREANISM Catherine Wilson
EPIDEMIOLOGY Rodolfo Saracci
ETHICS Simon Blackburn
ETHNOMUSICOLOGY Timothy Rice
THE ETRUSCANS Christopher Smith
EUGENICS Philippa Levine
THE EUROPEAN UNION Simon Usherwood and John Pinder
EUROPEAN UNION LAW Anthony Arnull
EVOLUTION Brian and Deborah Charlesworth
EXISTENTIALISM Thomas Flynn
EXPLORATION Stewart A. Weaver
EXTINCTION Paul B. Wignall
THE EYE Michael Land
FAIRY TALE Marina Warner
FAMILY LAW Jonathan Herring
FASCISM Kevin Passmore
FASHION Rebecca Arnold
FEDERALISM Mark J. Rozell and Clyde Wilcox
FEMINISM Margaret Walters
FILM Michael Wood
FILM MUSIC Kathryn Kalinak
FILM NOIR James Naremore
FIRE Andrew C. Scott
THE FIRST WORLD WAR Michael Howard
FOLK MUSIC Mark Slobin
FOOD John Krebs
FORENSIC PSYCHOLOGY David Canter
FORENSIC SCIENCE Jim Fraser
FORESTS Jaboury Ghazoul
FOSSILS Keith Thomson
FOUCAULT Gary Gutting
THE FOUNDING FATHERS R. B. Bernstein
FRACTALS Kenneth Falconer
FREE SPEECH Nigel Warburton
FREE WILL Thomas Pink
FREEMASONRY Andreas Önnerfors
FRENCH LITERATURE John D. Lyons
FRENCH PHILOSOPHY Stephen Gaukroger and Knox Peden
THE FRENCH REVOLUTION William Doyle
FREUD Anthony Storr
FUNDAMENTALISM Malise Ruthven
FUNGI Nicholas P. Money
THE FUTURE Jennifer M. Gidley
GALAXIES John Gribbin
GALILEO Stillman Drake
GAME THEORY Ken Binmore
GANDHI Bhikhu Parekh
GARDEN HISTORY Gordon Campbell
GENES Jonathan Slack
GENIUS Andrew Robinson
GENOMICS John Archibald
GEOFFREY CHAUCER David Wallace
GEOGRAPHY John Matthews and David Herbert
GEOLOGY Jan Zalasiewicz
GEOPHYSICS William Lowrie
GEOPOLITICS Klaus Dodds
GERMAN LITERATURE Nicholas Boyle
GERMAN PHILOSOPHY Andrew Bowie
GLACIATION David J. A. Evans
GLOBAL CATASTROPHES Bill McGuire
GLOBAL ECONOMIC HISTORY Robert C. Allen
GLOBALIZATION Manfred Steger
GOD John Bowker
GOETHE Ritchie Robertson
THE GOTHIC Nick Groom
GOVERNANCE Mark Bevir
GRAVITY Timothy Clifton
THE GREAT DEPRESSION AND THE NEW DEAL Eric Rauchway
HABERMAS James Gordon Finlayson
THE HABSBURG EMPIRE Martyn Rady
HAPPINESS Daniel M. Haybron

THE HARLEM RENAISSANCE
Cheryl A. Wall
THE HEBREW BIBLE AS LITERATURE
Tod Linafelt
HEGEL Peter Singer
HEIDEGGER Michael Inwood
THE HELLENISTIC AGE
Peter Thonemann
HEREDITY John Waller
HERMENEUTICS Jens Zimmermann
HERODOTUS Jennifer T. Roberts
HIEROGLYPHS Penelope Wilson
HINDUISM Kim Knott
HISTORY John H. Arnold
THE HISTORY OF ASTRONOMY
Michael Hoskin
THE HISTORY OF CHEMISTRY
William H. Brock
THE HISTORY OF CHILDHOOD
James Marten
THE HISTORY OF CINEMA
Geoffrey Nowell-Smith
THE HISTORY OF LIFE
Michael Benton
THE HISTORY OF MATHEMATICS
Jacqueline Stedall
THE HISTORY OF MEDICINE
William Bynum
THE HISTORY OF PHYSICS
J. L. Heilbron
THE HISTORY OF TIME
Leofranc Holford-Strevens
HIV AND AIDS Alan Whiteside
HOBBES Richard Tuck
HOLLYWOOD Peter Decherney
THE HOLY ROMAN EMPIRE
Joachim Whaley
HOME Michael Allen Fox
HOMER Barbara Graziosi
HORMONES Martin Luck
HUMAN ANATOMY
Leslie Klenerman
HUMAN EVOLUTION Bernard Wood
HUMAN RIGHTS Andrew Clapham
HUMANISM Stephen Law
HUME A. J. Ayer
HUMOUR Noël Carroll
THE ICE AGE Jamie Woodward
IDENTITY Florian Coulmas
IDEOLOGY Michael Freeden
THE IMMUNE SYSTEM
Paul Klenerman
INDIAN CINEMA
Ashish Rajadhyaksha
INDIAN PHILOSOPHY Sue Hamilton
THE INDUSTRIAL REVOLUTION
Robert C. Allen
INFECTIOUS DISEASE Marta L. Wayne and Benjamin M. Bolker
INFINITY Ian Stewart
INFORMATION Luciano Floridi
INNOVATION Mark Dodgson and David Gann
INTELLECTUAL PROPERTY
Siva Vaidhyanathan
INTELLIGENCE Ian J. Deary
INTERNATIONAL LAW
Vaughan Lowe
INTERNATIONAL MIGRATION
Khalid Koser
INTERNATIONAL RELATIONS
Christian Reus-Smit
INTERNATIONAL SECURITY
Christopher S. Browning
IRAN Ali M. Ansari
ISLAM Malise Ruthven
ISLAMIC HISTORY Adam Silverstein
ISOTOPES Rob Ellam
ITALIAN LITERATURE
Peter Hainsworth and David Robey
JESUS Richard Bauckham
JEWISH HISTORY David N. Myers
JOURNALISM Ian Hargreaves
JUDAISM Norman Solomon
JUNG Anthony Stevens
KABBALAH Joseph Dan
KAFKA Ritchie Robertson
KANT Roger Scruton
KEYNES Robert Skidelsky
KIERKEGAARD Patrick Gardiner
KNOWLEDGE Jennifer Nagel
THE KORAN Michael Cook
KOREA Michael J. Seth
LAKES Warwick F. Vincent
LANDSCAPE ARCHITECTURE
Ian H. Thompson
LANDSCAPES AND GEOMORPHOLOGY
Andrew Goudie and Heather Viles
LANGUAGES Stephen R. Anderson

LATE ANTIQUITY Gillian Clark
LAW Raymond Wacks
THE LAWS OF THERMODYNAMICS Peter Atkins
LEADERSHIP Keith Grint
LEARNING Mark Haselgrove
LEIBNIZ Maria Rosa Antognazza
LEO TOLSTOY Liza Knapp
LIBERALISM Michael Freeden
LIGHT Ian Walmsley
LINCOLN Allen C. Guelzo
LINGUISTICS Peter Matthews
LITERARY THEORY Jonathan Culler
LOCKE John Dunn
LOGIC Graham Priest
LOVE Ronald de Sousa
MACHIAVELLI Quentin Skinner
MADNESS Andrew Scull
MAGIC Owen Davies
MAGNA CARTA Nicholas Vincent
MAGNETISM Stephen Blundell
MALTHUS Donald Winch
MAMMALS T. S. Kemp
MANAGEMENT John Hendry
MAO Delia Davin
MARINE BIOLOGY Philip V. Mladenov
THE MARQUIS DE SADE John Phillips
MARTIN LUTHER Scott H. Hendrix
MARTYRDOM Jolyon Mitchell
MARX Peter Singer
MATERIALS Christopher Hall
MATHEMATICAL FINANCE Mark H. A. Davis
MATHEMATICS Timothy Gowers
MATTER Geoff Cottrell
THE MEANING OF LIFE Terry Eagleton
MEASUREMENT David Hand
MEDICAL ETHICS Michael Dunn and Tony Hope
MEDICAL LAW Charles Foster
MEDIEVAL BRITAIN John Gillingham and Ralph A. Griffiths
MEDIEVAL LITERATURE Elaine Treharne
MEDIEVAL PHILOSOPHY John Marenbon
MEMORY Jonathan K. Foster
METAPHYSICS Stephen Mumford
METHODISM William J. Abraham
THE MEXICAN REVOLUTION Alan Knight
MICHAEL FARADAY Frank A. J. L. James
MICROBIOLOGY Nicholas P. Money
MICROECONOMICS Avinash Dixit
MICROSCOPY Terence Allen
THE MIDDLE AGES Miri Rubin
MILITARY JUSTICE Eugene R. Fidell
MILITARY STRATEGY Antulio J. Echevarria II
MINERALS David Vaughan
MIRACLES Yujin Nagasawa
MODERN ARCHITECTURE Adam Sharr
MODERN ART David Cottington
MODERN CHINA Rana Mitter
MODERN DRAMA Kirsten E. Shepherd-Barr
MODERN FRANCE Vanessa R. Schwartz
MODERN INDIA Craig Jeffrey
MODERN IRELAND Senia Pašeta
MODERN ITALY Anna Cento Bull
MODERN JAPAN Christopher Goto-Jones
MODERN LATIN AMERICAN LITERATURE Roberto González Echevarría
MODERN WAR Richard English
MODERNISM Christopher Butler
MOLECULAR BIOLOGY Aysha Divan and Janice A. Royds
MOLECULES Philip Ball
MONASTICISM Stephen J. Davis
THE MONGOLS Morris Rossabi
MOONS David A. Rothery
MORMONISM Richard Lyman Bushman
MOUNTAINS Martin F. Price
MUHAMMAD Jonathan A. C. Brown
MULTICULTURALISM Ali Rattansi
MULTILINGUALISM John C. Maher
MUSIC Nicholas Cook
MYTH Robert A. Segal
NAPOLEON David Bell
THE NAPOLEONIC WARS Mike Rapport
NATIONALISM Steven Grosby

NATIVE AMERICAN LITERATURE Sean Teuton
NAVIGATION Jim Bennett
NAZI GERMANY Jane Caplan
NELSON MANDELA Elleke Boehmer
NEOLIBERALISM Manfred Steger and Ravi Roy
NETWORKS Guido Caldarelli and Michele Catanzaro
THE NEW TESTAMENT Luke Timothy Johnson
THE NEW TESTAMENT AS LITERATURE Kyle Keefer
NEWTON Robert Iliffe
NIELS BOHR J. L. Heilbron
NIETZSCHE Michael Tanner
NINETEENTH-CENTURY BRITAIN Christopher Harvie and H. C. G. Matthew
THE NORMAN CONQUEST George Garnett
NORTH AMERICAN INDIANS Theda Perdue and Michael D. Green
NORTHERN IRELAND Marc Mulholland
NOTHING Frank Close
NUCLEAR PHYSICS Frank Close
NUCLEAR POWER Maxwell Irvine
NUCLEAR WEAPONS Joseph M. Siracusa
NUMBER THEORY Robin Wilson
NUMBERS Peter M. Higgins
NUTRITION David A. Bender
OBJECTIVITY Stephen Gaukroger
OCEANS Dorrik Stow
THE OLD TESTAMENT Michael D. Coogan
THE ORCHESTRA D. Kern Holoman
ORGANIC CHEMISTRY Graham Patrick
ORGANIZATIONS Mary Jo Hatch
ORGANIZED CRIME Georgios A. Antonopoulos and Georgios Papanicolaou
ORTHODOX CHRISTIANITY A. Edward Siecienski
PAGANISM Owen Davies
PAIN Rob Boddice
THE PALESTINIAN-ISRAELI CONFLICT Martin Bunton
PANDEMICS Christian W. McMillen
PARTICLE PHYSICS Frank Close
PAUL E. P. Sanders
PEACE Oliver P. Richmond
PENTECOSTALISM William K. Kay
PERCEPTION Brian Rogers
THE PERIODIC TABLE Eric R. Scerri
PHILOSOPHY Edward Craig
PHILOSOPHY IN THE ISLAMIC WORLD Peter Adamson
PHILOSOPHY OF BIOLOGY Samir Okasha
PHILOSOPHY OF LAW Raymond Wacks
PHILOSOPHY OF SCIENCE Samir Okasha
PHILOSOPHY OF RELIGION Tim Bayne
PHOTOGRAPHY Steve Edwards
PHYSICAL CHEMISTRY Peter Atkins
PHYSICS Sidney Perkowitz
PILGRIMAGE Ian Reader
PLAGUE Paul Slack
PLANETS David A. Rothery
PLANTS Timothy Walker
PLATE TECTONICS Peter Molnar
PLATO Julia Annas
POETRY Bernard O'Donoghue
POLITICAL PHILOSOPHY David Miller
POLITICS Kenneth Minogue
POPULISM Cas Mudde and Cristóbal Rovira Kaltwasser
POSTCOLONIALISM Robert Young
POSTMODERNISM Christopher Butler
POSTSTRUCTURALISM Catherine Belsey
POVERTY Philip N. Jefferson
PREHISTORY Chris Gosden
PRESOCRATIC PHILOSOPHY Catherine Osborne
PRIVACY Raymond Wacks
PROBABILITY John Haigh
PROGRESSIVISM Walter Nugent
PROHIBITION W. J. Rorabaugh
PROJECTS Andrew Davies
PROTESTANTISM Mark A. Noll
PSYCHIATRY Tom Burns
PSYCHOANALYSIS Daniel Pick
PSYCHOLOGY Gillian Butler and Freda McManus

PSYCHOLOGY OF MUSIC Elizabeth Hellmuth Margulis
PSYCHOPATHY Essi Viding
PSYCHOTHERAPY Tom Burns and Eva Burns-Lundgren
PUBLIC ADMINISTRATION Stella Z. Theodoulou and Ravi K. Roy
PUBLIC HEALTH Virginia Berridge
PURITANISM Francis J. Bremer
THE QUAKERS Pink Dandelion
QUANTUM THEORY John Polkinghorne
RACISM Ali Rattansi
RADIOACTIVITY Claudio Tuniz
RASTAFARI Ennis B. Edmonds
READING Belinda Jack
THE REAGAN REVOLUTION Gil Troy
REALITY Jan Westerhoff
RECONSTRUCTION Allen. C. Guelzo
THE REFORMATION Peter Marshall
RELATIVITY Russell Stannard
RELIGION IN AMERICA Timothy Beal
THE RENAISSANCE Jerry Brotton
RENAISSANCE ART Geraldine A. Johnson
RENEWABLE ENERGY Nick Jelley
REPTILES T.S. Kemp
REVOLUTIONS Jack A. Goldstone
RHETORIC Richard Toye
RISK Baruch Fischhoff and John Kadvany
RITUAL Barry Stephenson
RIVERS Nick Middleton
ROBOTICS Alan Winfield
ROCKS Jan Zalasiewicz
ROMAN BRITAIN Peter Salway
THE ROMAN EMPIRE Christopher Kelly
THE ROMAN REPUBLIC David M. Gwynn
ROMANTICISM Michael Ferber
ROUSSEAU Robert Wokler
RUSSELL A. C. Grayling
RUSSIAN ECONOMY Richard Connolly
RUSSIAN HISTORY Geoffrey Hosking
RUSSIAN LITERATURE Catriona Kelly
THE RUSSIAN REVOLUTION S. A. Smith
SAINTS Simon Yarrow
SAVANNAS Peter A. Furley
SCEPTICISM Duncan Pritchard
SCHIZOPHRENIA Chris Frith and Eve Johnstone
SCHOPENHAUER Christopher Janaway
SCIENCE AND RELIGION Thomas Dixon
SCIENCE FICTION David Seed
THE SCIENTIFIC REVOLUTION Lawrence M. Principe
SCOTLAND Rab Houston
SECULARISM Andrew Copson
SEXUAL SELECTION Marlene Zuk and Leigh W. Simmons
SEXUALITY Véronique Mottier
SHAKESPEARE'S COMEDIES Bart van Es
SHAKESPEARE'S SONNETS AND POEMS Jonathan F. S. Post
SHAKESPEARE'S TRAGEDIES Stanley Wells
SIKHISM Eleanor Nesbitt
THE SILK ROAD James A. Millward
SLANG Jonathon Green
SLEEP Steven W. Lockley and Russell G. Foster
SMELL Matthew Cobb
SOCIAL AND CULTURAL ANTHROPOLOGY John Monaghan and Peter Just
SOCIAL PSYCHOLOGY Richard J. Crisp
SOCIAL WORK Sally Holland and Jonathan Scourfield
SOCIALISM Michael Newman
SOCIOLINGUISTICS John Edwards
SOCIOLOGY Steve Bruce
SOCRATES C. C. W. Taylor
SOUND Mike Goldsmith
SOUTHEAST ASIA James R. Rush
THE SOVIET UNION Stephen Lovell
THE SPANISH CIVIL WAR Helen Graham
SPANISH LITERATURE Jo Labanyi
SPINOZA Roger Scruton
SPIRITUALITY Philip Sheldrake
SPORT Mike Cronin
STARS Andrew King
STATISTICS David J. Hand

STEM CELLS Jonathan Slack
STOICISM Brad Inwood
STRUCTURAL ENGINEERING David Blockley
STUART BRITAIN John Morrill
THE SUN P. Gordon Judge
SUPERCONDUCTIVITY Stephen Blundell
SUPERSTITION Stuart Vyse
SYMMETRY Ian Stewart
SYNAESTHESIA Julia Simner
SYNTHETIC BIOLOGY Jamie A. Davies
SYSTEMS BIOLOGY Eberhard O. Voit
TAXATION Stephen Smith
TEETH Peter S. Ungar
TELESCOPES Geoff Cottrell
TERRORISM Charles Townshend
THEATRE Marvin Carlson
THEOLOGY David F. Ford
THINKING AND REASONING Jonathan St B. T. Evans
THOMAS AQUINAS Fergus Kerr
THOUGHT Tim Bayne
TIBETAN BUDDHISM Matthew T. Kapstein
TIDES David George Bowers and Emyr Martyn Roberts
TOCQUEVILLE Harvey C. Mansfield
TOPOLOGY Richard Earl
TRAGEDY Adrian Poole
TRANSLATION Matthew Reynolds
THE TREATY OF VERSAILLES Michael S. Neiberg
TRIGONOMETRY Glen Van Brummelen
THE TROJAN WAR Eric H. Cline
TRUST Katherine Hawley
THE TUDORS John Guy
TWENTIETH-CENTURY BRITAIN Kenneth O. Morgan
TYPOGRAPHY Paul Luna
THE UNITED NATIONS Jussi M. Hanhimäki
UNIVERSITIES AND COLLEGES David Palfreyman and Paul Temple
THE U.S. CIVIL WAR Louis P. Masur
THE U.S. CONGRESS Donald A. Ritchie
THE U.S. CONSTITUTION David J. Bodenhamer
THE U.S. SUPREME COURT Linda Greenhouse
UTILITARIANISM Katarzyna de Lazari-Radek and Peter Singer
UTOPIANISM Lyman Tower Sargent
VETERINARY SCIENCE James Yeates
THE VIKINGS Julian D. Richards
VIRUSES Dorothy H. Crawford
VOLTAIRE Nicholas Cronk
WAR AND TECHNOLOGY Alex Roland
WATER John Finney
WAVES Mike Goldsmith
WEATHER Storm Dunlop
THE WELFARE STATE David Garland
WILLIAM SHAKESPEARE Stanley Wells
WITCHCRAFT Malcolm Gaskill
WITTGENSTEIN A. C. Grayling
WORK Stephen Fineman
WORLD MUSIC Philip V. Bohlman
THE WORLD TRADE ORGANIZATION Amrita Narlikar
WORLD WAR II Gerhard L. Weinberg
WRITING AND SCRIPT Andrew Robinson
ZIONISM Michael Stanislawski

Available soon:

GEORGE BERNARD SHAW Christopher Wixson
ECOLOGY Jaboury Ghazoul
MODERN BRAZIL Anthony W. Pereira
SOFT MATTER Tom McLeish
PHILOSOPHICAL METHOD Timothy Williamson

For more information visit our website

www.oup.com/vsi/

Philip V. Bohlman

WORLD MUSIC

A Very Short Introduction

SECOND EDITION

OXFORD
UNIVERSITY PRESS

OXFORD
UNIVERSITY PRESS

Great Clarendon Street, Oxford, OX2 6DP,
United Kingdom

Oxford University Press is a department of the University of Oxford. It furthers the University's objective of excellence in research, scholarship, and education by publishing worldwide. Oxford is a registered trade mark of Oxford University Press in the UK and in certain other countries

First edition published 2002
This edition published 2020

Impression: 1

Published in the United States of America by Oxford University Press
198 Madison Avenue, New York, NY 10016, United States of America

British Library Cataloguing in Publication Data
Data available

Library of Congress Control Number: 2020932759

ISBN 978–0–19–882914–0

Printed in Great Britain by
Ashford Colour Press Ltd, Gosport, Hampshire

Once again, for my students,
generations past, present, and future,
from whom I have never ceased learning.

Contents

Preface

World music is very old and very new; it chronicles the ancient and the modern; it lives in the past and in the present. World music sounds the local and the global; it contains stories of the everyday and histories of epochs; it touches the most intimate parts of our lives and expresses the most transcendent qualities of human existence. World music is mobile and material; it circulates as mediated sound and affixes itself to the physicality of objects that sound; it at once encourages the desire and the denial of ownership. In all these ways, world music comes into existence because of its power to connect and to sound the common diversity of all human beings.

It is because of the vastness of world music that it has so many and such different meanings wherever we encounter it in the world. In this book I search for ways to account for the complex conditions whereby music has mapped and remapped the cultures of the world, in the past and in the present. There are many possible ways of defining world music, or laying claim to musical repertories as global, and it is these, considered as a whole, contradictions and all, that become the subject of this book. There are certain historical moments when definitions account for the presence of music in the world in specific ways. There is no clearer example of such a moment than Herder's coining of the term, *Volkslied*, or 'folk song', to account for a repertory he had gathered and published from global sources that together signalled a common humanity. Other definitions are more local and parochial, for example, when British record-company executives met in a London pub in the summer of 1987 to determine ways that the term 'world music' could provide a way of packaging and marketing the diverse genres of popular music that were increasingly appearing in their catalogues. 'World music' also gained definitional currency when applied to university programmes in ethnomusicology, designating 'centres for world music' and generating research programmes dedicated to world music as a subject matter. Definitions, then, also connected past to present in pursuit of commonality, even as the ways in which they sought connections across time and space.

The connections in which the definitions—and more critically, what I call the acts and conditions of world music—reside are critical to the structure of the present book. Each chapter contains a set of connections that realize the acts and conditions of world music at specific moments of globalization. In Chapter 1, we concern ourselves with the origins of world music, the acts and conditions that together sound various kinds of beginning—of myth and history, of religion, of discourse about the ontologies and epistemologies of music. Chapter 2 moves decisively toward history, focusing on the ways connections between the West and the rest of the world, especially the conditions of encounter, often result in the unequal distribution of power. Myth and history provide a framework for a wide array of connections in Chapter 3, between fundamental distinctions such as time and timelessness, oral and written tradition, concepts of listening in the Islamic world and of sounding music in Europe. Chapter 4 examines the most persistent model for world music, folk music, examining closely the conditions of its first appearance as a discourse of global musics, then following the history of that discourse. Similarly, the subject of Chapter 5, music and the nation, focuses on a specific set of conditions that have generated genres of world music that portray the nation and its insistence on a selfness distinguishing it from global partners. In Chapter 6 connections are at their most attenuated in the comparative study of diaspora and music, with examples drawn from the historical *longue durée* of diaspora as well as the dramatic proliferation of diaspora as a condition of modernity. World music is no less a presence when the connections are strained to the point of breaking in Chapter 7, which takes empire and globalization as points of departure, but moves critically through the potential of decoloniality to render connections anew. In the concluding chapter we search for new conditions of world music in the 21st century, especially the materiality affording new meanings that ensure world music matters in a changing world.

It is because world music matters that this book gathers perspectives that address the persistent presence of change as a condition of globalization connecting the past to the present. Change—historical, cultural, political, musical—is a crucial component of ethnomusicologal theory and method, especially the ways in which change is intersectional, transforming the musical objects (e.g. sounds and sites) to subjects and subjectivity (e.g. identity and epistemology). World music affords meaning to individuals and cultures in many ways, distinctive as they are different. Folk music may provide the conduit to world music for some cultures and communities, religious belief for others. World music is often intimate and personal, but it is no less often highly mediated and connected to virtual worlds. Its value may lie in the ways it is shared by a collective, or it may depend on the extent to which economic capital builds cultures of consumption with algorithms. World music is fundamentally material, while at the same time affording agency and mobility. It is the intersectional capacity of world music that lends it the particularly significant potential for analysing global change today.

The sections of this book that examine the most recent connections to a changing world engage the ways in which global history has itself undergone dramatic transformation, bringing about a cultural sea change. New areas of encounter between the West and former colonial regions, especially in the Middle East, North Africa, and their peripheral areas, such as Afghanistan and Somalia, have in recent years quickly passed from initial invasion to prolonged civil war and occupation. During the past decade movements on the right and the left arose in response to such encounters, soon thereafter unleashing new forms of global crisis, especially the forced migration of ethnic and religious minorities. Economic inequality and climate change further exacerbated the conditions undermining the global cultural unity in which world music participated and fraying the connections on which it depended.

The present edition of *World Music: A Very Short Introduction* is both a history of the present and a search for the presence of history in world music. The perspectives and approaches I muster in the following pages respond to different processes of change that have accelerated through history and generate the moment of globalization in our own day. It is critical for a book on world music to respond as extensively as possible to the sea change in global politics since the turn of the 21st century. The rise of right-wing populism, the spread of migration and refugee crises, and the escalation of climate change have global dimensions that are increasingly sounded in world music. The different case studies of music and musicians in this volume focus comparatively on the changing conditions in which world music comes into being and circulates. The various stages of the digital revolution, now a half-century old, have led to revolutionary transformations in the very ontologies and epistemologies of world music. Because of such transformations more people worldwide have greater access to world music than ever before in history. The traditional becomes the modern, the classical enters the everyday. Even at the moment the digital revolution opened new portals to music through the internet at the end of the 20th century, for instance, it would have been virtually impossible to predict that hundreds of performances of the same Hindustani *rāga* would be immediately accessible on YouTube, some of them claiming the potential to circumvent the traditional *guru-śiṣya parampara* of South Asian music. The increased digital mediation of world music notwithstanding, the present volume also recognizes the ways, often paradoxical, in which world music sustains the physical and material conditions that afford it ontological and epistemological presence in the lives of human beings. Several of the issues connecting the chapters of the book, such as music's mobility, extend traditional contexts to the present (e.g. the global refugee crisis), while others create bridges to problems whose urgency has become more acute than ever (e.g. climate change and cultural sustainability). By examining the many ways in which world music participates in change over time and sustains its critical presence in our own lived-in worlds, we witness the ways the past and the present enhance each other, as do the historical and ethnographic study of world music.

The historical and global landscape of world music is vast, encompassing the themes that coalesce as the many moments I investigate in the pages that follow. In order to clarify the ways the structure of this book represents such diverse moments of world music, I briefly sketch that structure here. The book unfolds as a series of thematic leitmotifs, each one forming a chapter. Though the chapter-length leitmotifs differ, their overall structures are similar, thereby making it possible to achieve an appropriately wide range of coverage. All chapters employ the same structure, that is, the same six sections through which I follow the leitmotif of the different chapters. Each chapter begins with an encounter, and it proceeds through a series of historical, theoretical, and aesthetic sections via vignettes of musicians and scholars before arriving at popular music and the present. Within each chapter I strive for internal consistency, returning in subsequent chapters to a point of beginning so that each chapter might become a narrative of encounter for the reader. The schema below summarizes the organizational structure of each chapter:

i: Encounter with world music
ii: Historical or theoretical excursus
iii: Profile of a musician or group of musicians
iv: Aesthetic issue, especially an examination of meaning and identity in music
v: Profile of an ethnomusicologist or group of scholars engaged with music globally
vi: Ethnographic present and popular music

Some of the encounters that fill the book come from my own experiences as an ethnomusicologist, especially those shaped by collaboration. They may come, more or less directly, from my own fieldwork; they may grow from historical and musical texts I have gathered over decades of archival work; they may represent, rather more indirectly, musical practices that I have experienced through theoretical engagement, for example my special concern with the relation between religion and music; they may resound with the lessons I have learned during the past two decades as an active performer, the Artistic Director of the New Budapest Orpheum Society; they may also arise from my own attempts to forge an approach that would enable me and, I hope, others to understand something of the whole of world music.

The first edition of this book was not initially my idea but that of George Miller, who at the time stewarded the Very Short Introductions through Oxford University Press. George put his faith in my ability to carry out the project, and I hope that, also in this edition, he might recognize my deep appreciation. I have been no less fortunate to have Jenny Nugee as the OUP editor for the present edition, above all because she has demonstrated such willingness to entertain many rather than fewer approaches to surveying the vast topics that typically become the subjects of Very Short Introductions. I wish also to thank Edwin Pritchard for his careful and thoughtful copy-editing. While thinking about the ways this book responds to music in a changing world I have benefited from the thoughts and ideas of several communities of readers and scholars who have critically engaged with the book. The first of these communities is that remarkable community I humbly and appreciatively recognize as 'my students' with the dedication to this book. Above all, my students have taught me that one indispensable goal of the book has been to encourage an inclusive and capacious attitude toward music. My planning for this book profited in ways I could not have predicted from the translators of its first edition—into Chinese, Hungarian, Italian, Japanese, Turkish, and Ukrainian—all of whom approached their task from the outset by seeking to make the book meaningful to the widest possible readership. I cannot thank you enough. My debt to two groups of colleagues, in Chicago and Germany, is enormous. What a marvellous community of ethnomusicologists we have had at the University of Chicago over many years: Jessica Swanston Baker, Melvin Butler, Travis A. Jackson, Kaley Mason, Ingrid T. Monson, Anna C. Schultz, and Martin Stokes. Over the course of recent years Berlin and Hanover have become my homes away from home, and I have therefore also accumulated the need to extend deep thanks to a host of German colleagues and friends, especially to Lars-Christian Koch, Raimund Vogels, and that non-Berliner Berliner, Fabian Holt.

At each of my personal and professional moments as a scholar of world music there is one thing that has remained forever steadfast: the abiding thanks to my family. As it does each time I bring a book to its close, the final word of acknowledgement here goes to Andrea, Ben, and Christine, now joined by Danielle and Riley, a marvellous collective of world and world-class musicians if there ever was one. Thanks for being there as we encountered music in the many places it has come to inhabit, wherever and whenever world music mattered so very much.

Philip V. Bohlman

Oak Park and Berlin

List of illustrations

List of maps

Chapter 1
In the beginning... Myth and meaning in world music

First encounters

First encounters with world music happen in many different ways. Some of us travel great distances to encounter music quite unlike anything we know from our home. Others first become aware of world music close to home, perhaps because of the arrival of immigrants or refugees from elsewhere, perhaps through an epiphany that the familiar was not what we had imagined it to be. For still others, first encounters come through recordings, internet links, or sundry forms of representation that draw attention to the distance between home and away, and possess the power to close that gap. First encounters with world music are often personal, even intimate experiences, engendering a sudden awareness of local knowledge. Such awareness seldom leaves us untouched, rather it transforms us, often deeply. In our different ways we may greet world music with awe and wonderment, fear and reverence; we may marvel at the serenity of its simplicity or the cacophony of its complexity; we may find ourselves lost in a search for meanings not immediately apparent but transformed through unexpected revelation. However and wherever first encounters take place, they profoundly change what we perceive music to be and how we understand its meanings in the lives of human beings.

First encounters are the stuff of story and history, thus they are of great interest for us in this book. Myth overflows with tales of first encounters. Just as myths tell about the intersections between the natural and the supernatural, or between humans and deities, so too do they account for how music emerges at those intersections. In myths supernatural beings often confer music upon humans as a gift. The gift may be abstract, opening a path to communication. It might also be concrete, for example in the forging of musical instruments from physical objects, such as human or animal bodies, which thereby acquire metaphysical meaning. Where music originates differs more in degree than kind in the myths of the world's religions. Music may be evident in the song of a bird or the voice of a god, or it may simply be 'out there' in the music of the spheres. Tales about the origins of music have a virtually universal presence in religions throughout the world, suggesting that mythological encounters may be among the first conditions of world music.

We also weave the stories about first encounters into the grand narratives that form our histories of world music. Let us turn briefly to one of the earliest of these stories. The first encounter between the musics of old and new worlds took place in 1557, during the sojourn of a Swiss Huguenot missionary, Jean de Léry (1536–1613), among the Tupinamba at what is today the Bay of Rio de Janeiro. In a 1578 account, Léry wrote extensively about the music of the Tupinamba, even including transcriptions of melodies and texts used in specific rituals, domesticating it as if, in his memory, they sounded more like European church music (Figure 1). Léry did not travel to the New World to write dispassionate, ethnographic observations, but rather to evangelize and convert, and his account therefore contains observations motivated by missionary zeal. The Tupinamba were cannibals, and the customs accompanying consumption of their fellow human beings especially caught Léry's attention. They also caught the attention of other writers of the day, not least among them Montaigne, whose essay 'On Cannibals', largely a series of

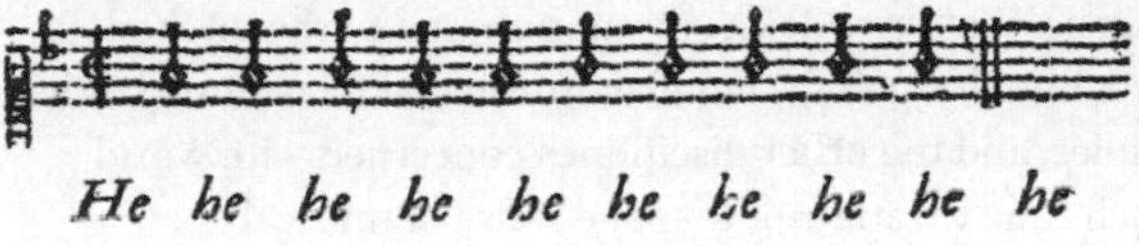

1. Jean de Léry's transcription of a Tupinamba melody (1578).

reflections on Léry's writings, led to wide dissemination of Léry's description of the first encounter. Léry's writings on Tupinamba music and their reception set a tradition of writing about world music in motion, a tradition that would accelerate through the Age of Discovery and the Early Modern era, culminating in Herder's late 18th-century collection of folk songs (see Chapter 2).

It is not even that Léry's account transformed a first encounter into an ethnographic moment that is important, but rather that he sensed the music of Tupinamba ritual was not so very different from the music of his own tradition, which he regarded as beginning with the Greeks and unfolding as Western music history. Léry described a process of growing closer to the music of the Tupinamba, undergoing an aesthetic conversion of his own, from an initial stage in which Tupinamba songs were meaningless to one in which he felt a closeness, even a recognizable kinship:

> At the beginning of this witches' sabbath, when I was in the women's house, I had been somewhat afraid; now I received in recompense such joy, hearing the measured harmonies of such a multitude, and especially in the cadence and refrain of the song.... Whenever I remember it, my heart trembles, and it seems their voices are still in my ears.
>
> (Léry, *History of a Voyage to the Land of Brazil*, 142 and 143)

It is in the nature of first encounters with world music that our memory of them produces an almost physical return to the encounter itself. This is the nature of musical ethnography, the common practices of physically being present when others are making music, that provides a common thread to the methods shared by ethnomusicology, popular-music and folk-music study, sound studies, and the other disciplines concerned with world music. Each time we attempt to make sense of musical phenomena differing from what is familiar, we return to first encounters, sometimes to retrieve information, but most often to remember again what it meant to experience world music for the first time. Reflecting on such encounters makes the best case for what happens when we experience world music, for, as in the case of Jean de Léry in the mid-16th century, transfiguration and transcendence, sometimes quite remarkable, accompany the encounter with music outside our own worlds, transforming it to world music.

First meanings of world music

One of the first things we learn upon encountering world music is that 'music' has different meanings elsewhere in the world. On one hand, music participates in cultural activities and connects to the world in ways unfamiliar to us. On the other, what is understood as 'music' itself might be entirely different, or what we think music to be might not be regarded as such. Knowing what music is and what it does may have little to do with categories that seem entirely natural to us. As we encounter world music, it is important to recognize the need to reckon with different epistemologies and ontologies if we are also to understand what world music can mean in its virtually infinite varieties.

By the epistemology of music we mean its ability to be a part of culture as a whole and thus to acquire meaning in relation to other activities. Examining music cross-culturally, we recognize that religious meaning accrues to music in many ways. Music may serve as a vehicle for shaping the voice of a deity; it may demarcate time so that it is more meaningful for the performance of ritual; music may provide one of many ornaments that make religious practice more attractive; certain domains of music-making (e.g. instrumental music in many religions) may raise images of magic or immorality, even causing some religions to prohibit music in worship. It is to understand such epistemological questions in world music more completely that ethnomusicology has adopted approaches from the social sciences, especially from anthropology, with its fundamental concern for cultural context.

The ontologies of world music—music's properties of being part of a lived-in world—are more likely to reveal themselves in musical texts and practice. The basic ontological question is simply, What is music? If the question is simple, the answers are not, for world musics have very distinctive and contradictory ontologies. From a Western standpoint, it often seems as if the ontologies of world music are untranslatable, especially because the most fundamental ontological categories in the West treat music as if it were an object, a 'thing' that itself possesses meaning. The language with which we talk about music and the ways in which we interpret it conspire to harden the objectified ontologies of our own music. An ontology derived from understanding music as an object is foreign to many music cultures in the world, where, for example, there may be no equivalent linguistic category for affording identity to individual pieces.

The most extreme instances of world music's ontological complexity are music cultures lacking a word equivalent to the Western concept of music. The musical culture of the largely Muslim Hausa people of northern Nigeria is a classic case of an ontology that contains a considerable vocabulary for distinguishing musicians, musical practices, and instruments, but no word for music itself. Clearly, the panoply of epistemologies and ontologies reveals itself in the ways we talk about music and the words we employ to give meaning to music. Box 1 contains a few of the countless terms used to ascribe ontological meaning to world music. The point here is not to suggest that such terms are equivalent to the Western 'music', but rather to urge readers to

Box 1 Ontologies of world music

ma: aesthetic emptiness and silence in Japanese music, perceived as an ontological entity in and of itself, rather than as a space (e.g. 'rest') between sounded music.

musica mundana: music of the spheres, a Neoplatonic concept employed by philosophers to account for music in the harmonic order of the universe.

ngoma: a concept encompassing a range of practices in the instrumental music of southern and eastern Africa. Glossed from the Bantu for 'drum' and 'drumming', ngoma further describes the social intersections of different genres and performance styles.

qirā'ah: recitation of the Qur'an, literally 'reading' or 'calling'. In Islam never considered to be music.

rasa: an emotional or spiritual condition in the music of South and South-East Asia—figuratively from the Sanskrit for 'taste, essence, mood'—attained by proper performance of various attributes, some musical and others extramusical.

samā': Arabic word translatable as both 'hearing' and 'listening'. Musical experience in Islam, determined by the perception of sound, rather than by its production.

saṅgīta: Sanskrit word roughly translatable as 'music', but in early theoretical treatises meant to embrace a range of practices that included Brahmanic ceremony, song, instrumental music, dance, and certain types of theatre.

soundscape: an overarching concept describing the acoustic spaces that give meaning to sonic phenomena, including music, but also ambient and environmental sound.

tarab: the emotional attributes of music, especially instrumental music, in the Arab world, achieved through a sense of feeling shared by musicians and knowledgeable listeners.

zikr: Arabic word translatable as both 'memory' and 'remembering'. Sufi ritual in which the Muslim believer draws spiritually closer to God by chanting the name of Allah with ever-increasing intensity.

question why seeking equivalent identities usually impedes discovery of deeper meanings.

The diversity of musics in the world has engendered its fair share of epistemological and ontological meanings, ranging from notions that music is fundamentally religious to the oversimplified pronouncement that music is a universal language. Such questions interest us throughout this book, not because we shall ever prove them correct or incorrect, but rather because they reflect a desire to endow music with global meaning. The desire to understand world music as revealing a pathway toward the universal is very powerful, so much so that it can have the inverse effect of creating the illusion that what we experience as world music is more similar than different. In the 21st century the search for common epistemologies and ontologies has both positive and negative implications for the ways we perceive the meaning of world music. Or do I mean for the meanings of world musics? The difference is not simply a matter of wordplay, for world music acquires meaning through both individual and collective, local and global, qualities, and sorting these out is anything but easy.

First musicians

Musicians, often in quite significant numbers, populate many mythological and religio-philosophical writings about the origins of religion and history—and music. When we reflect on the complex presence of music in epistemologies and ontologies of other human activities, it is hardly surprising that musicians should be there, indeed as what we here call 'first musicians'. These first musicians occupy the transitional spaces between what is not human and what is, and as musicians they appear in two guises, first as performers and second as craftspeople who fashion the musical instruments from the substance of the earth (see Chapter 8). First musicians appear at the mythological moments when identity is most critically called into question, particularly the identities that distinguish sacred from secular realms, and the natural from the artificial. In this way first musicians inscribe music upon the foundation myths of religions throughout the world.

Human intervention at the origins of music is no simple matter. In Jewish tradition there are two origin myths, both in the first book of the Torah, Genesis. In the fourth chapter, music comes into being associated with two different types of instruments, those made from the bodies of animals and shaped to resemble humans, and those moulded from the elements of the earth. One inventor of music, Yuval, is associated with the first, and another inventor of music, Tubal Cain, is associated with the second. Elsewhere in Genesis we encounter the ontology of music at the symbolic centre of one of the most far-reaching of all biblical stories, the *Akeda*, or 'Binding of Isaac'. In this story (Genesis 22) Abraham shows himself willing to carry out God's commandment to sacrifice his son, Isaac. As Abraham is about to kill his son, the voice of a messenger from God intervenes, informing Abraham that he may substitute a ram trapped by his horns in the nearby bushes. After Abraham has sacrificed and burned the ram, the animal's horns are left, and he rescues these to use them as the *shofar*, the sounding of which ritually and sonically represents Jewish identity, which remains traceable even today to the first musicians in Genesis.

Gods and goddesses, men and women assume many and varied forms throughout the great epic cycles of Hinduism, and we might assume—correctly—that the first musicians also play a significant number of roles. The first musician appearing with the greatest frequency, not only in the Hindu epic *Mahābhārata* but also in the visual iconography of music until the present, is Krishna. Krishna represents a constellation of divine qualities, among them divine love and beauty (*prema* and *rūpa*), but even more important for his role as a first musician is his association with *gopīs*, the female cowherds, which further symbolize the relation of the soul to god. That relation appears in countless images of Krishna playing the flute, in the narratives that accompany Indian modes, or *rāga*s, and iconography used to depict divine love.

Whereas Krishna's presence as a first musician is general, the goddess Sarasvatī enjoys a more localized presence, for example in the winter *pūjā*, or festival, bearing her name, which is auspicious for weddings (see Chapter 7). In Hindu writings she represents an ontology of human understanding, *vidyā*, that allows the human to transcend the cycle of reincarnation, and it is this ontology that she brings to the most primal of all Indian music instruments, the *vīṇā*. So basic is the meaning of the *vīṇā* to Hinduism that its very physical shape is regarded as metaphysically human. To enhance Sarasvatī's ability to effect *vidyā*, she appears frequently in iconography that appears on *vīṇā*s themselves; the *vīṇā* of Karnatak classical music, in fact, is often referred to as the *sarasvatī vīṇā*. Though a first musician of the first order, Sarasvatī retains her presence in Indian music today, serving as a reminder of music's first meanings (Figure 2).

Moments of beginning—religion, tradition, aesthetics

A revealed work itself, as written text, oral performance, and aural experience, the Qur'an is a revelation of the word of God. Meaning is immanent at many different layers in the Qur'an—the words and the written script in which they appear, the poetic form and the rhythm of the language, the modal and melodic patterns with

2. Sarasvatī with *vīṇā* in shrine, Bolpur, India.

which they are read and heard, aloud and internally. Perception and performance are conflated as experience in Surah 96, in which Muhammad hears the commandment of God through the revelation that Gabriel, as the messenger of God, reveals to the Prophet.

Read in the name of thy Lord who created,
Who created man of blood coagulated.
Read! Thy Lord is most beneficent,
Who taught by the pen,
Taught that which they knew not unto men.
(Qur'an, Surah 96: 1–5)

The Qur'an is a 'musical' work, which is to say that performance and perception depend on musical context, specifically the modal and melodic traditions of *qirā'ah*, the act of reading. The understanding of meaning is possible only through perception, namely through 'hearing' or 'listening' (*samā'*) to the revealed voice of God in the Qur'an's text. The aesthetic functions of the Qur'an, which are contingent on religious meaning, are ontologically not unique to it, and these lend themselves to comparison with other sacred texts. The recitation of the Qur'an also reveals something very basic about aesthetics in world music. In our encounters with world music, aesthetic issues cannot be bracketed off. The complex aesthetic embeddedness of world music is one of the ways in which it differs radically from Western music. Aesthetic embeddedness is strikingly evident in sacred music, where meaning is often dependent on music's ability to do something, to effect transformation or bring about transcendence.

Music possesses the aesthetic power to transform the material world into human experience, and it does so sweepingly at moments of beginning, enunciated by the earliest sacred texts of world religion. The transformation of the physical substance of the universe into the materiality of music—sound, movement, even melodic and rhythmic patterns manifested as musical scales—is explicit in sacred texts such as the *Rig Veda* of Brahmanic Hinduism, the 'Creation of the Sacrifice', which has been transmitted orally through written Sanskrit texts in India for over thirty-three centuries (Box 2).

Box 2 The Creation of the Sacrifice

The sacrifice that is spread out with threads on all sides, drawn tight with a hundred and one divine acts, is woven by these fathers as they come near: 'Weave forward, weave backward', they say as they sit by the loom that is stretched tight.

The Man stretches the warp and draws the weft; the Man has spread it out upon this dome of the sky. These are the pegs, that are fastened in place; they made the melodies into the shuttles for weaving...

The Gāyatrī metre was the yoke-mate of Agni; Savitṛ joined with the Uṣṇi metre, and with the Anuṣṭubh metre was Soma that reverberates with the chants. The Bṛhatī metre resonated in the voice of Bṛhaspati.

(*Rig Veda*, 1981: 31)

In Mahayana Buddhism of East Asia music transforms ritual into the political organization of monastic life, in which priests and lay people perform the meanings they encounter in a realm where both sacred and profane worlds overlap. As Pi-yen Chen has demonstrated, music realizes the ways in which individuals cohabit such worlds, allowing the worshipper to perform them simultaneously. We might imagine that all this is a lot to ask of music, but in fact the aesthetic embeddedness of music enjoins us to transform meaning through performance. The power of music in Buddhism, indeed in most religions, resides in the ways its meanings can effect transformation.

Ritual among Indigenous peoples throughout the world continues to bear witness to the ways in which musical meaning proliferates, producing multiple narratives that inscribe a long history of encounter. Christian hymnody for many Indigenous peoples of

North America has provided new possibilities for retaining Indigenous musical styles and performance contexts. The transformation of mission hymns to national anthems in Africa is yet another example of how the aesthetic embeddedness of music transforms meaning. Enoch Mankayi Sontonga's 'Nkosi sikelel'i Afrika' ('God bless Africa') first came into existence as a hymn, but underwent many transformations on its way to becoming a pan-African anthem of resistance to colonial domination and then a national anthem for Tanzania in 1964 and South Africa in 1995. In the course of its history, 'Nkosi sikelel'i Afrika' picked up texts in numerous Indigenous languages, as well as from the settler languages of English and Afrikaans, which together enhanced its post-colonial significance. As we expand our perspectives on world music, we begin to realize that the encounters producing it do not primarily create situations in which one side wins while the other loses. The aesthetic complex of world music requires a different set of perspectives, which together reveal music's myriad beginnings.

Charles Seeger, metaphysician of world music

Why choose Charles Seeger as a representative ethnomusicologist in this first chapter? After all, he was not only an ethnomusicologist, and his strong ethnomusicological leanings notwithstanding, he preferred to use the more inclusive 'musicology' to ethnomusicology, thereby signalling his unwillingness to eliminate any kind of music from an inclusive and 'unitary' field of musical study. It is not always easy to find common threads in the thinking and work of Charles Seeger, but it is the most common thread of all we explore here. In virtually all his writings on music, his activities as a teacher, and his undertakings as a public intellectual, Seeger concerned himself with the identity of world music.

Methodologically, philosophically, and musically, Charles Seeger (1886–1979) could not have been more eclectic. His musical education prepared him to be a composer, while his early predilection as a pedagogue led him to establish music within a broad liberal-arts curriculum. His first encounters with world music came later in his life, apparently after he discovered folk music as the 'music of the people'. His fieldwork was no less eclectic than his other undertakings, and though he engaged himself intensively with folk music collecting in the 1930s and 1940s, and then with Latin American music ethnography in the 1940s and 1950s, he largely turned from fieldwork to systematic approaches in the 1950s and 1960s, running experiments on the melograph, a mechanical device he created for transcribing musical sound recordings. Though his writings have the reputation for being enigmatic and he himself never fashioned a book from his diverse writings, Seeger influenced ethnomusicology in the 20th century like few other scholars.

There is, in fact, a discernible core to Seeger's thinking, and the eclectic paths of his diverse activities lead, rather consistently, to that core. In his writing we find an almost obsessive concern with one of the most basic ontological questions about music, its relation to words. Ultimately, this is a concern about musical meaning, the dilemma that arises when we must use words to talk about music even though words may fail to convey musical meaning adequately. Seeger's response to the dilemma was not to give up, but rather constantly to search for other ways to understand musical meaning. Social contexts were no less important than musical texts; ascribing value to different musics did not exclude the possibilities of measuring their physical and structural properties; recognizing the inadequacies of representational systems was no reason to forgo abstract models representing cognitive processes approximated by music. Seeger's influence on the study of music today confirms his vision that, with a growing awareness of world music's diversity, it would be possible for many to recognize the potential of becoming first ethnomusicologists.

In search of sacred beginnings—popular encounters with world music

World music has already produced its fair share of popular music stars, and more than a few have achieved mythical proportions. Stardom, in fact, may well form at the crossroads of a number of myths and mythologies, which together spread the popularity of world music during its *longue durée* and continue to do so in the 21st century. It was in search of the earliest star of the Sufi popular music, *qawwali*, that Ameera Nimjee and I entered the shrine complex of Hazrat Nizamuddin Auliya in Delhi in December 2014. The shrine complex contained the tomb of Amir Khusrow (1253–1325), a renowned musician, poet, scholar, and theologian of Islam, a Sufi in the fullest sense. Khusrow's life was one of mobility across the crossroads of North India, the Middle East, and Central Asia in the 13th and 14th centuries, an era during which the spread of Islam established itself after centuries of conflict in Pakistan and India, politically and culturally in the Delhi Sultanate.

Khusrow was a polyglot and a polymath, with vast knowledge of languages, literatures, and musical repertories, which he wove together through remarkable creativity. His poetry, his spiritual writing, and religious songs cohere in the musical style he is credited with founding, *qawwali*, a sacred popular music whose history stretches from the 13th century to the present. At our encounter in 2014, that history was fully evident, not only through the reverence of faithful pilgrims gathered about Khusrow's tomb, but also through the performance of *qawwali* ensembles that had travelled that night to the courtyard in front of the tomb (see Figure 3).

The several ensembles performing before Khusrow's tomb were both traditional and modern. They employed the familiar *qawwali*

3. Amir Khusrow's tomb in the Hazrat Nizamuddin Auliya, Delhi, India.

style of a solo singer and chorus, accompanied by a harmonium and the standard North Indian paired tabla drums. The clearly declaimed melodic line, frequently using call-and-response, made it possible for listeners not only to understand the song texts, but to join the ensemble on occasion, particularly at ecstatic moments. The crossroads of myth and history, too, demonstrated its material and metaphorical presence through the ways in which Sufism was a tradition unfolding across multiple directions of popular music. The mix of languages Amir Khusrow had woven into poetry and songs, among them classical forms of Persian and Urdu, had undergone a transformation to vernacular forms of Punjabi, Arabic, and Urdu. Above all, the popular *qawwali* style of the 21st-century Nizamuddin Auliya shrine captured the spirit of renewal and revival that has made Sufism popular through the countless world musics it has engendered.

As a complex of sectarian and communitarian practices within Islam, Sufism historically developed as a component of a world religion. Sufi sects formed wherever Islam spread, and for the most part these acculturated local musics were used in Muslim worship. Sufism embellished religious practice within Islam. In a religion that depends on the centralization of certain beliefs and sacred texts, Sufism formed at the peripheries, where it accommodated alterity and change. In the 21st century, in part as a component of Islam's political presence in post-colonial Muslim nations and in part because of the globalization of religion, Sufism has itself become a world religion. Sufism, in other words, is no longer solely a set of sectarian practices within Islam, but an expressive system throughout the world, the tenets of which can be embraced by Muslims and non-Muslims. Emblematic of this transformation is the frequent use of the term 'Sufi music' as a self-standing, aesthetic category of world music. The ontological and epistemological meanings of Sufi music as popular music at the beginning of the 21st century are fundamentally aesthetic.

Again, we witness the contradictions evident in the two different responses to globalization and world music. One set of perspectives welcomes the rise and spread of popular Sufi music as a historical process accompanying much that is about, say, religious revival in general and Islamic fundamentalism in particular. Another set of perspectives perceives negative implications in the same historical process. Is Sufi music a new music and an innovative set of practices with a traditional basis, or does it negate tradition by buying into the world music market? In the 21st century the historical trajectory of world music radically contrasts with the teleological history of Western art music—indeed, of the Euro-American mainstream in general—a history that unfolds through stylistic development and a genealogy of 'Great Men', each of whom passes the torch of tradition to a successor. In world music, tradition returns again and again, not to be used up or relegated to the past, but to be restored with new meaning in the present. As it becomes popular music, world music appropriates the past and tradition to effect a radical break with them. The great paradox—a paradox we follow through this book—is that popular music re-establishes the conditions of encounter because its historicity, marked by return and fuelled by revival, also reinstates encounter. Local musicians contribute to the forces of globalization, adapting the local and the traditional to shape the ontologies and epistemologies of world music in the 21st century.

Chapter 2
The West and the world

World music for the record

In the early history of folk music research and ethnomusicology, scholars doing fieldwork were often photographed organizing their collections and making their recordings. In several notable cases, these photographs have become icons for the collection and study of world music. There they are, the ancestors of today's ethnomusicologists and today's performers of world music, encountering each other and locked in the exchange of cultural knowledge. In Figure 4, the distinguished ethnomusicologist Frances Densmore (1867–1957), whose collections encompassed Indigenous peoples throughout North America, sits in 1916 with the Blackfoot, Mountain Chief, in Washington, DC, where he will sing to her, and she will chart his songs as traces on the map of Native American music. The recording session in Figure 5 depicts yet another level of and complicity in early ethnomusicological fieldwork, in this case conducted by Carl Stumpf (1848–1936) and Georg Schünemann (1884–1945), collecting the violin performance of a Tatar soldier who had been fighting for the Russian Empire before being captured and placed in a German prisoner-of-war camp.

Innumerable questions have been posed about such photographs, the representations of ethnographic encounter in the history of

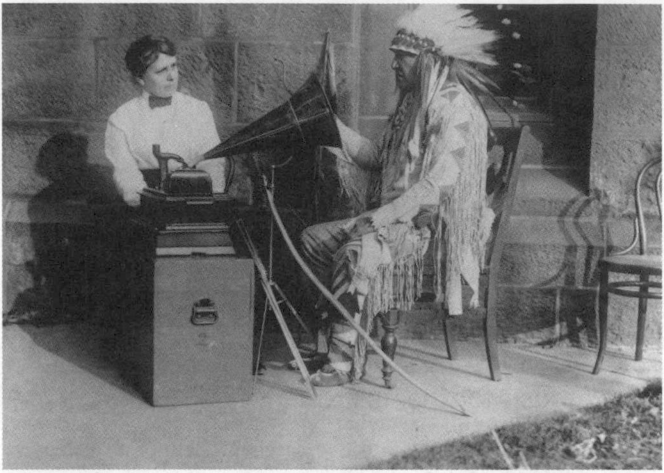

4. Frances Densmore and Mountain Chief, a leader of the Blackfoot people (1916).

5. Carl Stumpf and Georg Schünemann making field recordings of Tatar musicians in the Wünsdorf, Germany prisoner-of-war camp during the First World War.

world music. Are they meant to illustrate a sort of equality shared by fieldworker and consultant? Does the recording device separating them assure us of authenticity? What does the presence of mediating technology tell us about the 'fields' in which ethnographic encounter takes place? Are we witnessing a transfer of ownership, from musician to recording to transcription? The answers to these questions form an importunate narrative about the unequal distribution of power in the history of world music: the use of technological representation to appropriate music for the enjoyment, study, and consumption of those who do not own the music but do own the technology to possess it.

The critical examination of power—its use and abuse—lies at the heart of the present chapter. The unequal distribution of power forces us to confront the dilemma of ownership that arises when a transcription or recording of someone else's music appears as world music. Too often, through such acts of representation there is someone who gains power, while someone else loses it. Such discomfiting truths are anything but new. Indeed, they may be inextricably bound to the history and, more disturbingly, methodology of world music.

Recording and the audio moment

The ontologies and epistemologies of music undergo complex transformation in the process of recording, at the instance of the audio moment. The study of world music unfolds as an expansive field of audio moments, which together cohere as a historiography of sound recording itself. The guiding question for this historiography becomes, How does sound enter global history through acts of recording? The search for the audio moment follows diverse paths, in which the everyday and the historical *longue durée* converge. Audio moments, at the end of the nineteenth century, when the first recording technologies spread worldwide, proliferated across history as beginnings were repeatedly sounded. The repeatability of the audio moment is further remarkable because it is not ephemeral, fleeting, released from time, but rather it transforms sound into material, the very substance whose ontologies we experience as music.

The beginnings from which the audio moment is sounded spread across time and space, across religion and culture, musics and soundscapes. We witness audio moments in texts about beginnings, about sounding the universe in myth. They emerge from and then shape the meaning of the ontologies of the audio—as world music and as global history. The ontology of the audio is itself first observable at moments of beginning. The recording of music is only the most obvious ontology of the audio. Audio ontologies form around media such as film, theatre, and labour in private and public spheres. Together, all the senses shape listening ontologies as they enter the history of the senses.

The transformation of sound to society leads to what we examine in this chapter as the epistemologies of audio culture. The experience of listening results in very different social formations, from the most intimate spaces of prayer to the globalization of Bollywood soundtracks as world music. Audio epistemologies coalesce around the materiality of instrument building and the local and international patterns of exchange. Whether local, regional, or global, the epistemologies of audio culture are notable for the ways they afford connections and sound networks on many different levels.

The materiality of the audio moment is physical and tactile, at times an audio translation of the ontological and epistemological to the physicality of prayer, the sounding of bodies moving along the street, and the artifice of musical instruments. No less important for experiencing world music are the ways sonic materiality is intimate, concentrating the universal into the sound of the moment. The historical meaning that emerges from the audio moment is the result of specific acts and conditions, which together sound objects in order to afford meaning to the subjectivity of sound and the meaning of music. The acts and conditions of recording bring about transformations of many different kinds: authenticity is disrupted; some sound is amplified, some silenced; sound is given new life, even as salvage and sacrifice coincide. Music recording also produces a commodity that can be consumed. The acts and conditions of recording are thus varied, and music—especially world music, which fills the sonic space between local selves and global others—fills the audio moment to generate history. I now turn to these acts and conditions of the audio moment schematically, introducing them as processes of action and agency for sounding world music as global history.

Materiality. I begin with materiality because it provides both substance and metaphor for the sounding object. Material objects create and capture sound in accordance with specific physical properties. Just as sound begins with a material object, it is shaped by and then recorded by material objects that, in turn, give material substance to the audio moment.

Translatability. The second condition is translatability, which the reader should understand in the broadest sense possible. The processes accruing to the audio moment act on a sounding subject in ways that alter meaning, at the same time capturing as much meaning as possible. We translate by collecting and anthologizing, by locating recordings in a world of other recordings.

Transportability. The conditions of recording must allow for its transportability. The local becomes supra-local and, for the dissemination of world music, global. We act on the sounding object in ways that give it a place in the world: an archive, a wax cylinder, an MP3 file, a website.

Recording as technology. So obvious is it that we might overlook the omnipresence of technology as a condition for every act of recording. The audio moments that are important in a history of world music recording always accompany notable advances in technology. Advances in world music recording paralleled the histories of writing and speaking technologies that Friedrich Kittler traces through the 19th and 20th centuries, as well as the implementation of electronic microphones and the resulting recording revolution Michael Denning identifies in the late 1920s.

Collection as narrativity and historiography. The actions and agency of the audio moment transform collection to the conditions of history. As we look in this book at virtually any collection of world music, we find that the question of history looms large: Johann Gottfried Herder's folk songs, A. Z. Idelsohn's thesaurus of Hebrew melodies, Francis O'Neill's volumes of Irish folk song and dance from Chicago, all these collections are preoccupied with rescuing history before it becomes lost. It is these collections themselves that come to represent the world by juxtaposing its many dimensions.

Musicians of the Middle Passage

The world musicians I discuss at the midpoint in this chapter are by and large anonymous: I have little choice but to refer to them collectively as 'Musicians of the Middle Passage'. The Middle Passage was the geographical designation of the journey from Africa to slavery in North and South America, and in Europe and its colonies. The Middle Passage marked a space in which alterity was not just created but enforced through the cruelty of human trafficking and slavery. It was also a space in which world music was and, in the racial imagination, is forged.

Modern scholars are not without records of the musicians of the Middle Passage, but they were almost entirely written by individuals with names and power, for example ship captains, colonial officials, and missionaries. In contrast, the musicians themselves remain nameless and stereotyped, even though they frequently attracted attention through their propensity for music-making. The nameless musicians of the Middle Passage illustrate the ways in which the West has historically dominated by enforcing the anonymity of others. The music of the Middle Passage, too, remained nameless, characterized most often by stereotype and wanton misunderstanding. Much of the musical evidence from the Middle Passage survives only in the voices of those possessing the power to dominate, for example, in one of the best-known of all Christian hymns, 'Amazing Grace' (1779), a conversion hymn by a former slave trader, John Newton (1725–1807). Even when favourably described, the music of slaves was celebrated because the melodies were, as Alexander Barclay remarked in 1826, 'simple' and 'lively'. More often than not, those invested with more power to record the West in world history, such as G. W. F. Hegel, also writing in the mid-1820s, found it impossible to comprehend any such position for Africans:

> The African, in his undifferentiated and concentrated unity, has not yet succeeded in making this distinction between himself as an individual and his essential universality, so that he knows nothing of an absolute being which is other and higher than his own self.
>
> (Hegel, cited in Eze (ed.), *Race and the Enlightenment*, 127)

African music did survive the Middle Passage, and in the course of world music history, that music has influenced world music more than any other. Among the few possessions many forced to travel the Middle Passages were allowed to bring with them were musical instruments, and these were used to bridge the gap between Africa and the West. African musics developed into a boundless spectrum of genres and forms, through isolation of distinctive markers of selfness and the creative hybridization of otherness. As slavery was gradually eliminated over centuries, the musicians of the Middle Passage acquired new forms of mobility, recharting the vast region of the North and South Atlantic musically as the 'Black Atlantic', whose diverse patterns of global exchange remain evident in the popular music of the 21st century.

The West and the fissures between 'self' and 'other'

The space between the West and its others has vexed ethnomusicology since its inception. Depending on the historical moment and the disciplinary focus, it becomes the space between 'high' and 'low' culture, 'oral' and 'literate' culture, peoples 'with history' and those 'without history', 'premodern' and 'modern', or 'developing' and 'industrialized'. The paradox becomes even more troubling when we realize that all these conceptual pairs have distinctly Western origins. Within the pairs one term is available for the observer, transforming the other into a space occupied by the observed. The dilemma posed by the fissure between self and other is all-too-obvious because it is fraught with moral and ethical implications. For ethnomusicology the implications of the fissure are considerable. Ethnomusicologists cannot simply observe and describe the space between self and other, but rather they must enter it and deal with its complex forms of encounter. The space opens as the location in which fieldwork occurs. To enter the space between self and other is possible only upon acquiring power. Ethnomusicological encounter in the space, nonetheless, is distinctive because there has been considerable recognition of the implications of power for the exercise of praxis.

The history of ethnomusicology unfolds as a response to the dilemma posed by the fissure between the West and its others, by attempting to close it and even to heal the human devastation it sometimes causes. The point here is not to deny culpability for the abuses arising because of the fissure, but rather to suggest that ethnomusicology is notable for its recognition that closing the fissure has been a moral imperative. Attempts to redefine and close the space have produced a series of historiographical transformations, or paradigm shifts. One of the most sweeping of the early paradigm shifts was the direct result of Johann Gottfried Herder's publication of two volumes in 1778 and 1779, to which he gave the title *Volkslieder*, 'Folk Songs'. Herder argued that all people communicated through music as naturally as through speech. By gathering folk songs from as far afield as possible—quite deliberately from throughout the world—he created a space in which one cross-section of the world's music could symbolize a common humanity.

The space that a generalized concept of folk song could represent was enormously influential on following generations. In attempting to collect and publish folk songs to fill that space, however, Herder's successors in the 19th century sometimes hardened its boundaries, not least by claiming they expressed nationalist aspirations. The *Volk* of folk song ceased referring to 'people' and began to specify 'nation'. Whereas Herder did not attach the political-geographical designation 'German' to his 18th-century concept of folk song, it became the rule rather than the exception during the 19th century.

The employment of mechanical reproduction as a means of recording world music initially closed the gap. Almost from the first late 19th-century attempts to record world music on wax cylinders it became apparent that recording devices redefined the space between self and other. One could bring the 'field' to the cylinder recorder at world's fairs, or one could take the cylinder recorder to the field. Though massive in comparison to present-day digital recording devices, cylinder recorders were distinctive precisely because of their portability. They could, theoretically, capture music anywhere in the world, effectively negating the space between the West and its others.

The power of portable recording devices to collapse the difference between self and others is one of the mantras of globalization. Again, we witness the insistent presence of the key word, 'power'. In the opening decades of the 21st century, that persistence has not been lost upon a new generation of ethnomusicologists who are not themselves from the West and whose perspectives have coalesced in attempts to de-colonize fieldwork and the field.

Scholars working in these 'other ethnomusicologies' are not particularly sanguine about the potential of the field to heal such fissures. If the space between the West and its others will not close because it cannot close, it becomes incumbent upon ethnomusicologists to critique the very notions of selfness shaping their encounters with global others.

Johann Gottfried Herder and the invention of world music

With a single act of naming Johann Gottfried Herder (1744–1803) invented world music. It was Herder who coined the term *Volkslied* (folk song), applying it not only to the music he heard in the local world close at hand, but also to diverse repertories encountered throughout the 18th-century world. Herder imagined folk songs not only as discrete objects, the songs he published in two seminal volumes in 1778 and 1779, entitled simply 'Folk Songs', but also as a constitutive process of human subjectivity. In one of his most influential early writings on language, Herder held that the origins of speech and song were one, thus making music a distinctive characteristic of the culture all humans shared.

Would it be an exaggeration to describe Herder as an ethnomusicologist? He was, at the very least, a polymath, who was equally at home in theology, philosophy, linguistics, and anthropology, and his interest in music cut across the disciplines. The son of a Protestant church musician (*Kantor*) in rural East Prussia, Herder developed an early passion for church music and particularly local hymn-singing. He was not simply an amateur musician, for he collaborated with composers (notably J. C. F. Bach, a son of J. S. Bach) and court musicians by writing lyrics for them, and he incorporated musical themes into his own poetry, which then found its way into settings by many composers, among them Beethoven, Schubert, Brahms, and Richard Strauss. The first traces of what would become a sustained interest in folk song are evident in his 1770 meeting and collaboration in Strasbourg with Goethe, who was at the time gathering Alsatian folk songs. Herder himself took a special interest in folk songs from the peripheries of Europe, and traditions from the Baltic lands—his first pastoral position was at the cathedral of Riga, Latvia—occupy a very visible position in his collections.

Herder's role as an inventor of world music has acquired further significance because of its influence on several critical areas of Enlightenment thought and then beyond on Romanticism. To Herder are attributed several fundamental critical formulations of nationalism. His seminal translation of the Spanish epic, *El Cid*, became a model for the publication of national epics across the world during the 19th century. Herder's writings about music are remarkable for their expansiveness. At the moment of encounter, he wrote during an extended journey across the Baltic and North seas in 1769, 'I wish to collect data about the history of every historical moment, each evoking a picture of its own use, function, custom, burdens, and pleasures.' If the map he sketched for his philosophy of history emanated from his vantage point as a European intellectual, it nonetheless stretched across the entire world.

Recording and the anthological impulse

With the final section of this chapter I turn to a set of related case studies that provide answers to the two questions about power that recording the musics of other cultures consistently raises. Though the primary actors constituting the dramatis personae in these recording projects are connected through the network provided by an institution dedicated to the recording, preservation, and understanding of world music, the Berlin Phonogram Archive (founded 1900), the recording projects they undertook expose fundamentally different models of world music, models already evident in the first printed anthologies of world music (e.g. Herder's two volumes of folk songs) and in the most recent anthologies of world music, released on CDs or through the internet, consumed for educational and entertainment value.

The first two anthologies examined here together constituted the first attempts by an ethnomusicologist to respond to what I call the 'anthological impulse': gathering together diversity on record in order to represent world music in a holistic way. Although Erich Moritz von Hornbostel (1877–1935) organized and edited—anthologized, one really should say—both projects, they differ in some very distinctive ways. In the most basic sense the two anthologies have different audiences, which is also to say different consumers. The basic differences motivating the anthological impulse have continued to characterize world music recording and collection up to the present.

If we think of Hornbostel's *Demonstration Collection* (1963, orig. 1910s and 1920s) and *Music of the Orient* (1979, orig. 1934) as the 'first anthologies on record', it is to make some larger points about the anthological impulse as a persistent theme in the history of world music. That theme draws our attention to a number of issues having to do with mediation: between collector and collected; between those unable to represent themselves and those with the economic and technological capital to do so; between humanistic fascination and exotic fantasy. Hornbostel's anthologies together made an important first step toward using the anthology for more than archiving field recordings, making them available (1) to scholars for study and (2) to a broader audience for popular consumption.

The Demonstration Collection *and* Music of the Orient. The scientific and the popular often split into two sides separated by a mediational divide. On one side we witness the primary concerns of the early comparative musicologists. The anthologies contain examples that clearly served as gateways to understanding music's origins and authenticity. The listener navigates the anthology using a comparative map; at every outpost something new accrues to the world music traveller's knowledge of music's immanent diversity. It was the goal of the anthologizers to use music to chart global maps in new ways. On the other side of the mediational divide we witness the representational language of *fin-de-siècle* fantasies of the exotic, for the anthologies are also repositories of strangeness, whose attraction is their absence of familiarity. The maps of world music constructed by the two Hornbostel anthologies look quite different. The *Demonstration Collection* views world music from the bottom up; *Music of the Orient* views world music from the top down. In the first anthology we encounter a welter (42 from the original anthology of *c*.120) of very brief examples, often performed by anonymous performers at the farthest reaches of ethnological study. Even the examples from Europe come from repertories that were regarded as very old and prehistorical (e.g. track 1 is Swiss yodelling, and track 3 comes from the Caucasus). Distinguishing the 'Orient' on the second anthology are practices of art music, which require the greater sophistication of larger ensembles and longer works. There are fewer examples (24), among them two shellac recordings, and many are extracts or movements from larger works.

Both anthologies bear witness to historical concepts, but history in the *Demonstration Collection* begins primarily with the oldest—and by extension most authentic and exotic—examples and unfolds along a path toward greater complexity. In the second anthology Hornbostel follows the Orientalist model of history, which Hegel and 19th-century European historians had systematized, in which 'civilization' moves from the East to the West. World music history in the first anthology is inclusive, embracing the most isolated music cultures in Oceania and the *longue durée* of European traditions. On the second anthology music narrates an exclusive world history for the Orient, moving along a single path on which progress is intrinsic to separating people with history from those without history.

The *Demonstration Collection* is inclusive in another way: it includes the work of scholars, as well as of colonial officials and missionaries, who were committed to documenting the earliest forms of music and then transforming these into comprehensive scientific discourse. We note such discourse in the use of transcriptions of music, text, and ritual with quite exacting ethnographic and musical detail.

There was no equivocating when it came to stating that the goals of *Music of the Orient* were different from those of the *Demonstration Collection*. By the early 1930s, monographs and more popular studies of world music were appearing in significant numbers, spurred on by the popularization of humanistic scholarship in general. Recordings had won a new place in the public sphere during the 1920s, creating new audiences who possessed gramophones in their homes. *Music of the Orient*, released on the Odeon and Parlophone labels (at the time German and English transnational recording labels), deliberately took advantage of these several transformations in music consumption. *Music of the Orient* told a different story with world music, and it did so by anthologizing in a different way, exemplified in Figure 6, an 'art-song' from Tunis, in '*maqām mezmūm*'.

In more ways than one way, the two recorded anthologies represent African musics that were geographically, ontologically, and historically unlike each other. Whereas the *Demonstration Collection* places considerable emphasis on sub-Saharan Africa, an object of colonial desire for Germany, *Music of the Orient* considers only North Africa. The site of collecting for the former is the 'field' and 'mission station', but the site of collecting in North Africa is 'the town', the cosmopolitan centre where both Andalusian (i.e. quasi-medieval European) and modern European (i.e. the violin, which Hornbostel assures the reader is 'European') influences mix with the 'ancient view of life'. In both cases the musicians are travelling along a historical track that brings them

Tunis

23. Art-song. *Maqām Mezmūm*

The ancient view of life places the life of man as well as all earthly events—microcosmos—in counter-relation to a path of deified stars, seasons and hours of the day—macrocosmos. The music, too, is included in the harmony of the cosmos; the harmony adopts the personality of the planetary deity represented in the leading tone; this type of composition demands a proper time and occasion of delivery in order to bring about bliss and not destruction. Maqām Mezmūm calls the demons—but woe if the call resounds inside the house!

The ancient faith and customs have, in the "Andalusian" style—originating in the Moorish Period of Granada—been more purely preserved in the north-western towns of Africa than in the East. This Tunisian recording belongs to this style. A European violin alternates with the vocalist in the melody, a lute ('Ud) accompanies (see recording 19). The metrically timed song is preceded by a rhythmically free structure, which displays the characteristic feature of the Maqām: the leading tone at the base of the structural treble (Do-Modus), the accentuated "Neutral" third (halving the treble) and principally the fundamental theme:

Tonal structure *:

Town Players. Photo: Dr. R. Lachmann.

6. 'Art-song' from Tunis, in *maqām mezmūm*.

close to the West, either through conversion to Christianity in sub-Saharan Africa or through the demolition of the borders between Europe and North Africa in the Tunisian art-song, which would play an important role at the 1932 Cairo Congress of Arab Music (see Chapter 3).

The First World War 'Royal Prussian Phonographic Commission' and Robert Lachmann's 'Oriental Music Broadcasts'. The scholars and scientific institutions engaged in early recording projects were wont frequently to take advantage of the encounter that accompanied war, especially along the borders of empire, where global history was particularly exposed. Among the first ethnographic accounts of world music *in situ* were the voluminous publications of the French scientific commission that followed Napoleon into Egypt at the beginning of the 19th century, led by Guillaume-André Villoteau (1759–1839). Similarly, in the 1940s, musicologists commissioned by the Japanese army, occupying Taiwan as a colony at the time, made extensive recordings of the music of ethnic and Indigenous groups on the island. It should not be surprising, therefore, that the ethnomusicologists associated with the Berlin Phonogram Archive should recognize the anthological impulse that arose during the First World War and on the eve of the Second World War, albeit under vastly different conditions.

The First World War collecting endeavour took place in German prisoner-of-war camps that held captives from the largely colonial lands whose residents were mustered to fight against the German, Austro-Hungarian, and Ottoman empires. Africans fought for England and France, as did soldiers from the Middle East and South Asia. The Russian imperial army had called Jews and Koreans to military service, as well as diverse nationalities and religions from the Caucasus and Central Asia. Created in 1915, the Royal Prussian Recording Commission set out to gather as many recordings of music and speech as possible, eventually amassing some 1,022.

Among those collecting in the German prisoner-of-war camps was the comparative musicologist, Robert Lachmann (1892–1939). We have occasion to meet Lachmann on numerous occasions in the course of this book (see especially Chapter 3)—as one of the founders of modern ethnomusicology and Jewish music research, as the head of the scientific commission at the 1932 Cairo Congress of Arabic Music—but here we primarily concern ourselves with the anthological impulse behind the 'Oriental Music' radio broadcasts he created in Jerusalem. With limited means after settling in Jerusalem—German recording companies denied him the materials necessary for wax-cylinder recordings—Lachmann turned to makeshift technologies (e.g. field recordings inscribed on discarded celluloid X-rays) to gather music from throughout mandatory Palestine, designed to reach a

7. Cover of *Music! The Berlin Phonogramm-Archiv 1900–2011 in 111 Recordings* (2011).

general public through recordings and lectures on the radio. That these in themselves constitute a remarkable microcosm of world music is clearly evident in Ruth Davis's 2013 publication of them in digitized sound format and transcriptions.

Postscript—Music! *2011*. One of the most remarkable traits of the anthological impulse is its persistence over time, hence its inseparability from ongoing histories of world music. In 2011, the Berlin Phonogram Archive, centrally involved in the recording projects we have been tracing through this chapter, released a five-CD set entitled *Music! The Berlin Phonogramm-Archiv 1900–2011 in 111 Recordings*. It is clear already from the cover of the anthology (Figure 7) that *Music!* represents a recorded history of recording, conscious attention focused on the ways scholarly concerns intersect through ethnography and performance. Ethnomusicologists and musicians cohabit the spaces of world music. (CD 5 even contains four 'field recordings' of my cabaret troupe, the New Budapest Orpheum Society, made while on tour in Berlin in 2009 and 2013.) In the historical moments that unfold across the tracks of the Berlin Phonogram Archive's *Music!*, the materiality with which the anthological impulse underlies the history of world music recordings could not be more tangible.

Chapter 3
Between myth and history

Who owns the future?—The 1932 Cairo Congress of Arab Music

For a month during the spring of 1932 Cairo, Egypt, became the epicentre for debates about the position of Arab music in world music. The brainchild of Maḥmūd Aḥmad al-Ḥifnī (1896–1973), the Congress of Arab Music gathered the greatest scholars and musicians from Europe and the Arab world, stretching from Morocco in the west to Iraq in the east. Al-Ḥifnī, who held the position of 'Inspector of Music' at the Egyptian Ministry of Education, enjoyed the strong backing of King Fu'ād and the Academy of Oriental Music in Cairo. The Congress would be a grand event, 'an East-West encounter', as A. J. Racy describes it, on the highest musical plane.

The goals of the 1932 Congress of Arab Music were ambitious and had all the trappings of an encounter that would change world music history. The Europeans were invited to the Congress not only to witness the past but also to provide expert advice for the future. The list of musical and ethnomusicological dignitaries was stellar, including the composers Paul Hindemith and Béla Bartók, orientalists such as Baron Carra de Vaux and Henry George Farmer, and ethnomusicologists such as Curt Sachs, Erich Moritz von Hornbostel, and Robert Lachmann. The delegations from

North Africa and the Levant brought music ensembles, whose concerts would bear witness to lavish government support. There were celebrities among the musicians as well, for example the Iraqi singer Muḥammad al-Qubbānjī, and, unknown to the participants, there were also a few would-be stars, notably Umm Kulthūm of Egypt. The Congress marked an auspicious moment for encounter in world music.

All did not turn out as expected, but perhaps that too should have been expected. The Europeans and the Arab delegations brought with them quite different expectations about the future of Arab music. We might have expected that the Europeans would argue for a historical agenda of change: was it not high time to untether Arab music from past glories so that it could flourish again? Similarly, we might have expected the Arab delegations to showcase the past and make a case for preserving it. Just the opposite was the case. Recognizing the indebtedness of European music to the great traditions of North Africa and the eastern Mediterranean during the Middle Ages, the Europeans took a stance on the side of tradition. Tradition, however, meant that European and Arab music stood apart in world music history; it meant that they were different, and that they belonged to two distinctive historical epochs, one—Arab music—prior to modern history and the other—European music—coeval with modernity.

The Egyptians responded with respect to the European tradition. Whereas Arab pride in the greatness of the past was palpable, the more visible agenda was modernity. How might the past serve as a springboard for the future? How might modern Western instruments be transformed for Arab music, say by retuning the piano for microtonal modal systems? How might recording and publishing projects disseminate Arab music globally?

Clearly, the European and Arab delegations had two vastly different worlds in mind. For the Europeans it was the world of the past, in which Arab music had arguably been dominant, but also a world frozen at great distance from the present. The European position bore all the earmarks of what Edward Said called 'orientalism'. The orientalist 'East' was transformed by the European gaze into an object at which one might marvel, but also an object helpless against the intervention of the West. The magnificence of Arab music lay in its historical inertness, in the fact that its narrative had been closed.

The Arab delegations wanted to engage with world history anew, and they were unwilling to accept the orientalist arguments for historical closure. World music, as they wished to confront it, allowed change and was not irreconcilably stuck in the past. Behind their interest in change was the interaction between history and the nation-state. The government agencies in Egypt, from King Fu'ād down, recognized that modern nation-states laid claim to national cultures. The nationalist agenda was clear also in the musical delegations, which represented 'nations' not 'cultures' or even 'traditions'.

In the history of world music during the 20th century, the 1932 Cairo Congress of Arab Music stands as a watershed characterized by paradox. For many Arabic music scholars the Congress marks the moment at which Arab music history re-entered world music history. The Congress also serves as a reminder that what gets admitted to the canon of world music depends on many factors, at once historically contingent and contradictory.

Mediating the medieval—North Africa in the history of world music

In the imagination of world history North Africa has long been the *locus classicus* of in-betweenness. Geographically, North Africa is connected by the Mediterranean to Europe, but separated from the rest of Africa by the Sahara. Historically, much that provided cultural foundations for Europe started in North Africa, for example the influence of ancient Egypt on Classical

Greece and Rome. Theologically, the Abrahamic faiths of Judaism, Christianity, and Islam all remained indebted to North Africa. The classic land of encounter, North Africa continues to sustain ongoing encounter in the 21st century.

In the Middle Ages it was North Africa not Europe that could claim dominance on the stage of world history. It was North African Islam rather than European Christianity that supported cultural advances—in science, medicine, and the arts—with truly global proportions from roughly the 9th century CE until the Renaissance. The inventor of world history—historiography with the world as its subject—was North African, the 14th-century polymath Ibn Khaldūn (1332–1406). Today, we know Ibn Khaldūn as an intellectual able to do it all. He was a diplomat whose posts took him from Spain to Damascus. He was a devout Muslim, hence his religious views are particularly revealing of Islam. He was a writer of history, who endeavoured in the 1370s to write a history of the universe, a task so sweeping that he completed only the 'introduction', the *Muqaddimah*.

Ibn Khaldūn also turned his attention to world music. Viewed from the perspective of ethnomusicology today, he was very modern, even if we do not necessarily agree with all his findings. He wrote, for example, that different cultures had different musics, and he attributed this to, among other things, the impact of climate. He argued that music could influence human actions in profound ways, for example spurring peoples to go to war, but music was also anchored in elaborate theoretical systems. As a Sufi, Ibn Khaldūn also recognized there was much about music that humans could not understand because of music's sacredness. Music appears, throughout the *Muqaddimah*, inseparable from Ibn Khaldūn's view of world history.

Whatever its presence in the history of the world, the music of medieval North Africa was essential to the formation of European music. Muslim theorists working in Arabic and Latin, such as al-Fārābī (872–950) and Ibn Sīnā (980–1037; better known by his Latin name, Avicenna), wrote works seminal to thinking about music in Europe's Christian monasteries. So powerful was the global influence of North Africa that later generations often overlooked the presence of Arabic music in European music. Take the instrument of measurement in Arab music theory, the *'ūd*, whose strings allowed theorists to explain the physics of sound, while demonstrating the auditory traits closest to the human voice. We can trace that instrument from the eastern Mediterranean, where its name, *al-'ūd* (the wood), followed it across North Africa with Islam to the Iberian peninsula, where it was altered in Spanish and Portuguese to forms of *la-ute*, which then underwent further modification to '*Laute*' in German and 'lute' in English.

North Africa contained not a single music culture but many. In addition to the presence of classical Arab musics, which produced both instrumental and vocal canons, such as *ma'lūf* in Tunisia, North Africa was home to countless dialects of vernacular music, such as the sacred practices of *stambeli*, with its complex web of rituals from Islam and sub-Saharan migrants. The nomadic peoples of the region, such as the Bedouins, have long possessed rich narrative traditions, not least among them the great *hilali* epic cycles. In the western parts of North Africa, the 'Maghreb', Islamic musics mixed with Christian and Jewish traditions, producing one of the greatest of all hybrid classical traditions, Andalusi music. In the wake of the *reconquista*, which led to the expulsion of Jews and Muslims from Spain and Portugal in the 1490s, North Africa quickly gave rise to new classical and hybrid traditions, especially those in the Judaeo-Spanish songs of the Sephardic Jews.

The encounter with Islam, North Africa, and the Middle East is everywhere in European music from the 18th century to the present. Whether in opera libretti from Mozart to Verdi or in the wind and percussion sections of the modern orchestra, Western music has gathered elements of the Islamic world, leading many musical scholars to take it upon themselves to determine what North Africa had given to Europe. The musical scholar Guillaume-André Villoteau (1759–1839), for example, accompanied the scientific team that Napoleon packed off to Egypt, later publishing two encyclopedic volumes on the music of Egypt. As Europe intensified its colonialist interventions across the Mediterranean, musical scholars were there, gathering and systematizing more evidence that would allow them to cast the music of the 'other' as their own. Scholars and writers turned their gaze toward North Africa, often leaving us with some of the most penetrating descriptions of music, for example in the novels of Gustave Flaubert and in the stories of Paul Bowles. The in-betweenness of the music of North Africa did not escape them, because they themselves were critical factors in the calculus of that in-betweenness.

Umm Kulthūm—a star is born

There are those who would say that Umm Kulthūm (1904–75) was the most popular singer of the 20th century. Statistically, it would be hard to refute such claims. Umm Kulthūm enjoyed success as a recording artist, making an estimated 300 recordings in her lifetime. It is surely the case that wherever one purchases recordings in the Islamic world—the marketplace of North African towns, CD shops in the Muslim neighbourhoods of Paris, or airport electronic shops in Indonesia—there will be a surfeit of Umm Kulthūm recordings. During the last part of her career in Egypt Umm Kulthūm was perhaps best known for her radio and television broadcasts, which together constitute a national myth about Egypt's collective response to Umm Kulthūm's voice. In Egyptian films her status as an icon—as a woman, a musician, and an Egyptian—extended beyond Egyptian society to global cinema.

Umm Kulthūm's iconic presence in world music is not without paradox. Her life as a singer was in many ways traditional. She came early in life to singing, albeit within a strictly Muslim context. Her father was the local *imam*, the leader of the village mosque, and at the age of 5 she began to attend the village religious school. It was here that learning was based on recitation of the Qur'an. Already as a girl Umm Kulthūm joined her father at weddings and religious festivities, where he sang semi-professionally. Thus, as she learned to sing, she also acquired a repertory of sacred song.

In every respect traditional song provided the basis for Umm Kulthūm's style. We might ask whether she became a famous singer despite the restrictions of tradition. The ways she employed mode, or *maqām*, were anchored in the recitation of the Qur'an. Prosody and poetic patterns owed their form and articulation to sacred texts. Even the relation of her voice to the small orchestras accompanying her revealed her unwillingness to abandon fundamental Muslim aesthetics.

The distinguished biographer of Umm Kulthūm, Virginia Danielson, provides us with a forceful counterargument, namely that it was because of the contexts of tradition that Umm Kulthūm became a figure of international proportions. Danielson writes that 'to be a listener to Umm Kulthūm was to join many others in a validation of a communal social universe'. The world that Umm Kulthūm's songs evoked was not primarily global but local, but its many different forms were palpable in the lives of listeners throughout the world. It both substantiated the aesthetic resonance of sacred song in the present and carved out new political potential for tradition in a changing world, thereby giving voice to women and the popular ethos of the modern Muslim world.

Islam and the meaning of music

Were we to have been flies on the wall at the 1932 Cairo Congress, listening to the Arab delegations debating their agendas, to the Europeans trying to find a common scientific language, and to

Umm Kulthūm conversing with her instrumentalists about which songs would best represent their tradition, we probably would have wondered if they were all talking about the same thing. It would not only have been a matter that different terms were applied, but that some terms were avoided or used with studied obliqueness. Umm Kulthūm, very likely, would not have referred to her singing as 'music', reserving that term for her instrumental ensemble. If the Europeans had pressed the Arab musicians to provide practical examples of theoretical concepts, the musicians would have wondered what the foreigners meant by confusing theory and practice. We were not flies on the wall at the Cairo Congress, but we do know that it produced little agreement on anything. Such results were inevitable in Cairo in 1932 because of the complex ways it is possible to talk about music within Islam—or not to talk about music.

Complicating the discourse about music in North Africa and the Mediterranean are the questions arising from Islamic attitudes toward music. These attitudes range from contentions that Islam condemns music altogether to claims that Islamic writings are ambivalent toward its practice. Two primary literary sources are traditionally used to understand music's acceptability: the Qur'an and the interpretive works concerning the Prophet Muhammad's teachings, called *aḥādīth* (commentaries). Neither source is unequivocal in its pronouncements concerning music. The Qur'an contains *suwar* (chapters; sing. *sūrah*) that seem to condone activities associated with music, as well as *suwar* cited as evidence that Muhammad condemned music. Even these primary writings do not address music per se but rather cultural activities with which music might be associated, such as poetry or dance. It is hardly surprising, therefore, that modern positions toward music vary greatly. The *aḥādīth* also frequently originated in lands conquered during the spread of Islam, and they therefore initially reported on cultural activities in didactic ways only. As Islam spread across North Africa, music was extrinsic rather than intrinsic to its concerns.

In the course of Arab music history musical terminology increasingly framed distinctions between what was inside and outside Muslim society. Recitation of the Qur'an (*qirā'ah*) and the call to prayer (*adhān*) were not considered musical activities at all, but rather practices designated as 'reading', one of the literal meanings of *qirā'ah*. The role of music in reading religious texts is that of enhancing meaning through clarification. It is this role that provided the basis of Umm Kulthūm's 'musical' education. What to the Western observer sounds like music is secondary to textual projection and religious expression.

Once attention turns to instrumental genres, the terminology of musical discourse suddenly bears witness to foreign concepts. One encounters, for example, the widespread use of the term *mūsīqā* (or *mūsīqī*), borrowed from the Greek language. Properly used, *mūsīqā* could never apply to *qirā'ah* or *adhān*. Among the Islamicate sciences that flourished in the Middle Ages, *mūsīqā* designated the presence of foreignness. Terminological distinctions were used to calibrate cultural distance, as in describing secular music that is strictly vocal as *ghinā'* (song). When Ibn Khaldūn wrote about song and instrumental music in the *Muqaddimah*, he did so in entirely different chapters. It was hardly surprising in the 20th century that the delegations at the Cairo Congress found themselves talking about vastly different phenomena. Such distinctions were even greater in modern colonial contexts, where Western 'music' had acquired many of the same associations with foreignness. From an Islamic perspective such differences were prerequisites for talking about world music at all.

The gaze of ethnomusicology—Robert Lachmann in North Africa

The 1932 Cairo Congress was not the first orientalist excursion into North Africa for all the participants. Robert Lachmann (1890–1939), the senior music librarian for the Berlin Prussian

State Library and editor of the most prestigious journal in comparative musicology, *Zeitschrift für Vergleichende Musikwissenschaft*, had made several research trips in the 1920s. Because of this experience he was chosen to head the German delegation and to serve as the official reporter for the Europeans at the Cairo Congress. When he first visited North Africa in the 1920s, Lachmann imagined himself taking a journey into Europe's past, where he would find music that had not changed for centuries. What Lachmann expected to find and what he found were two different historical phenomena. During one extended field trip to Tunisia, Lachmann made the decision to focus on the old Jewish communities on the island of Djerba, located in the Mediterranean off the coast of Tunisia. Djerba had all the trappings of an 'isolated' music culture. Because of the great age of the Jewish communities, two villages with several hundred souls each, Djerba might also add considerable evidence to the theories about the preservation of music prior to the destruction of the second temple in Jerusalem (70 CE). He sought not so much a 'missing link' as the introductory chapter in the music history from Antiquity to the present.

The music Lachmann collected on Djerba, however, left little doubt that it was more modern than ancient. First of all, though most sacred music, such as that in the Djerba synagogues, was clearly Jewish because of Hebrew texts and ritual functions, it sounded like the music of Muslim villages in Tunisia. Second, the instruments and modal structures of much secular music were indistinguishable from other Tunisian styles. Third, the music of Djerba's Jewish women was virtually identical to many Muslim vernacular repertories. It would be impossible to claim that Djerba's music had remained 'Jewish' by surviving in isolation. Lachmann was not deterred, and he asked how the conditions leading to hybridity might have come about. By carefully analysing the music, he found his answers. Djerba, though geographically isolated, was on an important pilgrimage route across North Africa. Jewish and Muslim pilgrims sojourned on the island, and when they departed, they also left traces of their music. Even more significantly, Jews, Muslims, and others on Djerba and the Tunisian mainland shared a common musical life, and exchange was more often the rule than the exception.

The last decade of Lachmann's life was marked by many of the tragedies that befell German-Jewish intellectuals. When the Nazis seized power in Germany in 1933, he was dismissed from his librarian's post. Because of his activities as a scholar and editor—and also because of his important role at the 1932 Cairo Congress—Lachmann was able to gain support from the young Hebrew University for moving many collections in his sound archive to Jerusalem, where he laid the foundations for modern Israeli musicology. When we listen to the radio broadcasts of music he delivered before his death in 1939, published by Ruth Davis in a modern edition, we witness Lachmann's portrayal of the musical worlds of North Africa and the eastern Mediterranean as modern. The music of North Africa proved not to be primarily a link to the past, but rather it was the Cairo Congress and Lachmann's Djerba research that formed a link to the present.

Bereshit/In the beginning—Mediterranean epic from myth to history

Epic arises from the Mediterranean as song shaped by the sea, as history formed by the myths told of the peoples, cultures, and religions traversing its coastlines through time. The journeys of the heroes who give their names to Mediterranean epic—Moses in the Five Books of Moses, or Torah, in the Bible, Ulysses/Odysseus in the *Odyssey*, the Cid in the national epic of Spain—navigate and narrate the stretch of the sea that gives the Mediterranean its name, lying 'between the lands'. When the great Mediterranean epics are sounded through song, their journeys, in the 21st century as in Antiquity, pass from myth to history. Mediterranean epic contains the spirit of great faiths, particularly the Abrahamic faiths of Judaism, Christianity, and Islam. The epic of Moses, the Torah, chronicles a common ancestry—*bereshit*, 'in the beginning' (Box 3)—whereas the *Kosovo Cycle* of south-eastern Europe chronicled the battles against the Ottoman Empire in the 14th century as tales of irreconcilability.

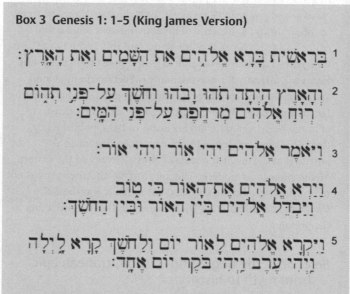

Box 3 Genesis 1: 1–5 (King James Version)

1 בְּרֵאשִׁית בָּרָא אֱלֹהִים אֵת הַשָּׁמַיִם וְאֵת הָאָרֶץ׃

2 וְהָאָרֶץ הָיְתָה תֹהוּ וָבֹהוּ וְחֹשֶׁךְ עַל־פְּנֵי תְהוֹם
רוּחַ אֱלֹהִים מְרַחֶפֶת עַל־פְּנֵי הַמָּיִם׃

3 וַיֹּאמֶר אֱלֹהִים יְהִי אוֹר וַיְהִי אוֹר׃

4 וַיַּרְא אֱלֹהִים אֶת־הָאוֹר כִּי טוֹב
וַיַּבְדֵּל אֱלֹהִים בֵּין הָאוֹר וּבֵין הַחֹשֶׁךְ׃

5 וַיִּקְרָא אֱלֹהִים לָאוֹר יוֹם וְלַחֹשֶׁךְ קָרָא לָיְלָה
וַיְהִי עֶרֶב וַיְהִי בֹקֶר יוֹם אֶחָד׃

English translation

1 In the beginning God created the heavens and the earth.
2 The earth was without form and void, and the darkness was upon the face of the deep; and the Spirit of God was moving over the face of the waters.
3 And God said, 'Let there be light'; and there was light.
4 And God saw that the light was good; and God separated the light from the darkness.
5 God called the Light Day, and the Darkness he called Night. And there was evening and there was morning, one day.

As a narrative genre that itself comes into existence as poetry and music, performed by the poet-musicians long populating the Middle East, North Africa, and southern Europe, epic has acquired the attributes of a simulacrum virtually inseparable from the Mediterranean and the religions shaping its long history. Epic provides the template for creation and foundation myths stretching from one end of the Mediterranean to the other. Through each retelling and resinging, myth becomes story becomes history becomes modernity. What served Moses as the 'Promised Land' in the Torah became a historical model for the State of Israel. The sovereignty of the Spanish region of Castile for the Cid provided a template for national independence not only for medieval Spain, but also for Latin American nationhood during the 19th century.

The nations and worlds separated by the Mediterranean also find their way into the musical structure of epic. The duality of the two worlds separated by the sea is realized in the hemistiches—the two-phrase lines separated by a poetic break, or caesura—that dominate the structure of Mediterranean epic. It was the generative function of the two hemistiches in Balkan epic that provided two of the great 20th-century epic scholars, Milman Parry (1902–35) and Albert B. Lord (1912–91), with a theory of oral transmission in Lord's book, *The Singer of Tales*, which has influenced the understanding of epic globally. The great translators of Balkan epic in south-eastern Europe—among them, Johann Gottfried Herder, Vuk Stefanović Karadžić (1787–1864), Béla Bartók—seized upon the caesura as the site for musical translation and historical imagination.

If I attribute considerable influence to the intimate relation of epic to the Mediterranean and the transformation of myth to the histories of modern nations, I am hardly the first to do so. Homer and Herder, the chroniclers of the Torah and the North African Beni Hilal epic, all endowed epic with the power to narrate the emergence of national sovereignty in history. The translations of epic singers and epic scholars alike realized that epic draws us into nation-states larger than life, places of sovereignty beyond the lands occupied by mere mortals. It is the power of epic as one of the oldest and most widespread genres of world music that sustains it as the avatar for the human journey from myth to history, in the present as in the past.

Chapter 4
Music of the folk

Folk music between myth and history

Folk song and folk music might well constitute the original world music, the mother lode in a historical tradition connecting music to global phenomena. As a music shared by the many rather than the few, folk music has a universal presence. It is a premise of folk music scholarship that every human being has access to repertories of folk music, those that distinguish intimate groups as well as those with traits believed universal. The connections between the intimate and the universal, as between the local and the global, afford folk song and music the power to speak to and for the masses, the *Menge* in Johann Gottfried Herder's paean to the music of the folk, 'song loves masses'. The search for folk music, thus, begins at home, but it leads inexorably to the global, to the musical practices expressing the basic humanity of culture.

Folk song and the non-vocal forms of folk music emerge from the many aspects of culture that human communities share and that shape the everyday. A community's folk song, therefore, coheres around a common language, in which the myths of the past enter the expressive practices of the present. Folk dance affords a community social interaction in physical, public ways. Sacred folk music enables a community to weave a shared belief system into liturgy and ritual. The relation between community, commonness, and communication is essential to folk song and folk music, connecting repertories in oral tradition to practices enhancing literacy, and linking the local to the global. Folk music is therefore dynamic, and it enhances the ways in which communities change.

The discourse about folk music derives from an impulse to imagine world music. When Johann Gottfried Herder, writing from the heart of the Enlightenment, coined the term *Volkslied* (folk song), he deliberately documented it with examples from throughout the world (see Chapter 2). Herder's folk songs possessed national attributes, and they both shored up and transgressed linguistic borders. Herder imagined a distribution of folk song as world music that was equally capacious and generous.

If folk music made it possible to imagine the world musically, it did so according to a particularly European perspective. When European scholars identified folk music beyond Europe's borders, it more often than not resembled European folk music. Mobility was one of the most frequent attributes of folk music, empowering scholars to scour the globe for the migrations of entire peoples. At the same time, mapping the world with folk music had all the earmarks of colonialism. If the collection of folk music was implicated in European encounters throughout the world, it came increasingly to reflect the ideologies of modernity, not just colonialism but also nationalism and the search for authenticity. Folk music attracted the political left no less than the political right; it became an emblem of modernity and provided a vocabulary for its malcontents.

The cultural space of folk music responds to two broadly conceived sets of metaphors, the first temporal and the second spatial. The temporal and spatial metaphors of folk music are interdependent and intersectional. In many different ways folk music proclaims rather loudly that it is about place. Song texts identify the location in which they take place, usually in the first line or two, and dance forms use movement to outline spaces of narrative action. The quintessential rural Alpine folk dance, the *Ländler*, not only comes from the 'land', but in its original versions makes it possible for dancers to act out with dance 'figures', or stylized gestures, their relationship to life in the mountains of Central Europe. The intersection of narrative and geographical qualities made it possible to make claims on that space. Folk music's narrative and geographical qualities coalesce in such ways that they allow a collective metaphorically to enter the cultural spaces evoked, opened, and then represented by folk music. Bartók realized this when he collected folk songs from the Hungarian regions of Romania and Slovakia. So, too, did the generations of German scholars who mapped the 'folk-song landscapes' of so-called *Sprachinseln* (linguistic enclaves).

The cultural spaces of European folk music are and have been ceaselessly contested, often within a single song or dance. Real and imagined spaces appear, and the characters of the song struggle to occupy the spaces, metaphorically representing the struggle for place and history. We might take as an example the Yiddish folk ballad 'Hinter Poilen wohnt a Yid' (Beyond Poland there lived a Jew). Even at the most local levels the narrative of the song reveals a struggle for space. The daughter in an observant Jewish family challenges her parents as well as her community by asking to enter the public spaces beyond traditional community life. Both her parents and European history deny access to that public space, for it was not until the mid-19th century that European Jews were permitted to own land. The more local issue, especially in the version in Box 4 of a ballad with Jewish and non-Jewish variants (e.g. in the first canon of German folk poetry, *Des Knaben Wunderhorn*, and in a setting by Johannes Brahms), is the requirement that the daughter convert. Few variants of the folk song, which stretch from the Middle Ages to the present, resolve the dilemma posed by the conflict between real and unrealizable spaces; in many variants, the Jewish girl chooses suicide rather than conversion.

Box 4 'Hinter Poilen wohnt a Yid' [Beyond Poland there lived a Jew]

Beyond Poland there lived a Jew
With a marvellous wife;
Her hair was beautifully braided,
Just as she was beautifully made-up;
And she danced wonderfully.

Mother, dearest mother,
I have such a headache;
Let me go for a little while
For a walk on the street!
• • •

The mother went to bed,
The daughter jumped from the window;
She jumped over the iron fence,
Where the scribe was waiting for her.

Scribe, you dearest,
Scribe, you who are mine,
How can that be possible?
—If you let yourself be baptized,
You'll be called Mary Magdalene
And you'll be my wife!

'Hinter Poilen wohnt a Yid' is a Yiddish variant of the High German ballad, 'Die Jüdin' ('The Jewish Woman', DVldr 158), published in the earliest anthology of Yiddish folk songs from Russia (Ginsburg and Marek, *Evreiskie narodnye pesni v Rossii*, 313–14). Translation from the original Yiddish by Philip V. Bohlman.

Folk tales of two cosmopolitans

In Budapest, until the 21st century one of the most cosmopolitan of former imperial metropolises in East Central Europe, folk music historically enjoyed pride of place. The scholars of Hungarian folk music have acquired the status of national culture heroes. In the first half of the 20th century the composers Béla Bartók (1881–1945) and Zoltán Kodály (1882–1967) were known as ethnomusicologists *and* composers, whereby their nationalism and modernism were welded into a single cultural identity. Bartók and Kodály were neither the first nor last Hungarian composers to take an active and activist interest in folk music. Folk music embodied and grew from a musical discourse of Hungarianness, and the stakes of that discourse were very high, for they raised questions not only of ethnic identity, but also of racial purity and of national integrity.

In the Kolkata of the 21st century, similarly a cosmopolitan centre of empire from the time of its establishment as Calcutta by the English East India Company at the end of the 17th century, song in many forms, especially in the genres bearing Bengali lyrics from the Ganges flood plain, symbolically sounded the journey from a classical past to a global modernity. Bengal, before its partition into two parts, East and West, today the nation of Bangladesh and the Indian state of West Bengal, had been an extensive region of rural settlements, through which multiple traditions of music flowed. Traditional sacred musics sprang forth from the diverse sources of Hinduism and Islam, with Sanskrit, Persian, and Urdu texts, but then drew upon common Bengali texts and heterodox, syncretic religious practices, especially Vaishnavism and vernacular forms of Sufism. Folk music found its roots in the countryside, but flourished because of the cosmopolitanism of empire.

When Bartók is portrayed among the pantheon—usually at the centre of that pantheon—of great Hungarian musicians, it is almost inevitably with photographs that represent him as a cosmopolitan folk music collector (Figures 8 and 9). In Figure 8, we witness Bartók accompanied by his cylinder recorder in a Slovak village, with a line of peasants waiting to sing for him. In

8. Béla Bartók collecting folk songs in Zobordarázs (Dražovce), Slovakia (1907).

Figure 9, Bartók sits at his desk, this time with his ear turned towards a gramophone horn. Folk songs entered one recording horn, and they issued from the other. The two recording horns symbolize the modernity of authenticity, but they make even clearer the intervention of ideology at the expense of authenticity. The stages of mediation could not be more evident. Song emanates from the women who had never left the village, symbols of authenticity. At the national centre, in the urbane culture of modern Hungary, the authentic was recovered, but only after a chain of recording and transcription.

Rabindranath Tagore (1861–1941) assumed his place in the pantheon of Bengali culture heroes by charting paths to the folk both similar and different from Bartók's. Raised amidst the urbane intelligentsia of Calcutta, Tagore drew from the confluence of the arts both modern and global. As a creative figure, he was a polymath who seemingly knew no bounds to the expressive

9. Béla Bartók with gramophone.

practices at his command; he was a painter and a poet; he was a mystic philosopher and a novelist, indeed, achieving the honour of being the first Asian to receive a Nobel Prize (1913, Literature).

Tagore was also a folklorist, singer, and composer, and these are the roles that are particularly important for his contributions to world music. The cosmopolitan world of 19th- and 20th-century Calcutta notwithstanding, Tagore's journey to the music of Bengal took him on a journey to the countryside of the Ganges flood plain, to the lyrical and melodic vernacular that connected human experience to nature. Tagore remained far closer to oral tradition than Bartók, never fully embracing the recording technologies or employing the exactitude of transcription. He freely transformed the songs that he either collected or created. Tagore was one of the first to recognize the beauty and significance of the Bāul and Bôyāti musicians, whose musical practices grew to be virtually synonymous with a Bengali folk music that unites East and West Bengal (see Chapter 8).

In the course of his lifetime, Tagore would create some 2,200 songs, which symbolically cohere in an eponymous style and repertory important for all Bengalis as *rabindrasangeet*, 'Rabindranath song', which he published in the two volumes called *Gitabitan* (Song offerings), and which appeared in 1942, the year following his death. In the 21st century, *rabindrasangeet* continue to represent a canonic Bengaliness, whether in the entire sections dedicated to them in CD shops, or in the ethnomusicological research of scholars such as Lars-Christian Koch. Like the compositions of Bartók, the songs of *rabindrasangeet* convey the possibilities of a modernity arising from folk music. Unlike Bartók, Tagore stopped short of an aesthetic of modernism, investing a different form of complexity in the songs he gathered along the tributaries of Bengal, past and present. Significantly, however, both Bartók and Tagore were prescient in their recognition of the ways folk and world music had long shared common borders.

Leadbelly and the making of a folk musician

No folk musician did more to raise the profile of folk song in America during the first half of the 20th century than Huddie Ledbetter, generally known as Leadbelly (1885–1949). Leadbelly became an icon for what folk music had been prior to modernization, in the African American culture of the 19th-century South, and for what it would become once discovered by collectors, scholars, and record companies. Born in rural Louisiana, Leadbelly acquired his musical skills early in life, picking up the twelve-string guitar he used to accompany a repertory estimated at 500 songs. As a young man, he rambled between jobs in Louisiana and Texas, between the cotton fields and the oil fields. Leadbelly's life was one of plying the boundaries between an anachronistic past and an oppressive present. He also served time in various prisons, not just for misdemeanours, but also for several serious felonies, among them murder (1918–25) and attempted murder (1930–4). It was while serving time in the Louisiana State Penitentiary for the second of these felonies that John Lomax 'discovered' Leadbelly, a fully-fledged blues singer, suitable for presenting to the Library of Congress.

There can be no question that Leadbelly played a crucial role in the transformation of African American folk music to world music, particularly in the subsequent generations of folk music revival. As his two names symbolized, Leadbelly shifted between several identities. As 'Leadbelly' he played the blues and attracted the attention of scholars—not just the Lomaxes (discussed below) and Seegers (see Chapter 1), but ethnomusicologists and record producers, notably Moses Asch at Folkways Records. 'Huddie Ledbetter' was both more ancient and more modern than Leadbelly, signalling a deep-rooted connection to rural Southern songs and providing the official name he used as singer-songwriter-composer of a prodigious number of songs (e.g. 'Rock Island Line', 'Midnight Special', 'House of the Rising Sun', and 'Good Night Irene') that became hits in their day and anthems for revivals in the decades to come. Disentangling myth from history in Leadbelly's biography is quite impossible.

Why would we, however, need to disentangle myth from history? That the 'folk music' Leadbelly performed both was myth and was invented to serve as myth goes without saying. As a consummate performer, Leadbelly recognized that his anachronistic blues style might appeal the most to northern white liberals, but that a more eclectic fusion of black song styles might win him audiences in New York City jazz clubs. With his music he could evoke and even reify a constellation of cultural spaces, some representing moments in his own life—the Great Migration, the Great Depression, and the Second World War. He could talk with and through those who recognized his potential as maker of myths and chronicler of history. Whatever the mix of myth and history in

Leadbelly's life, folk music won a much greater place in both because of that life.

Celtic music and the regional cartography of folk music

How does folk music become world music? Does it lose its attributes as folk music once it circulates globally? Does it become popular music when performed globally in music festivals or television series? Or art music when providing composers with the raw material for new compositions? Few other musics yield answers to these questions more directly than Celtic music. There are few places in the world where Celtic music has not made its presence known. It is hard to imagine a metropolis anywhere in the world that does not have at least one pub or tavern hosting live Celtic music. Celtic music is a staple of world music festivals. The phenomenal global success of Celtic music, nonetheless, depends on its capacity to retain its folk roots.

Myth, history, and the politics of modernity intersect in Celtic music. In its global forms as world music, Celtic music relies on the myths it narrates about itself. Myth, however, is very modern; Celtic music locates it in the distant past. Archaeologists have long thought of the Celts as a Bronze Age culture that spread across the whole of Europe; they were proto-European Europeans, a fact derived from Antiquity that bolsters claims of modernity. As the Romans pushed northward into Europe during the first centuries of the Common Era, Celtic tribes initially offered stiff resistance, but then retreated to the northern and western fringes of Europe, lands that remained Celtic and autochthonously European until the present.

Histories of Celtic peoples stress their unity, a unity that, too, has acquired mythical proportions. Language is one of the most frequently extolled myths of unity. The two major Celtic-language families, the Goidelic and the Brythonic, bear witness to cultural survival and the ability of native speakers to maintain them. Religion, too, has mixed myth and history to underscore unity, for 'Celtic religion' has acquired a double meaning, on onc hand, a pagan, pre-Christian past, preserved archaeologically in the stone evidence for cultic practices, and on the other, the historical practices of Christianity, which followed distinctive musical routes in the Middle Ages, for example when St Patrick brought Catholicism to Ireland in the 5th century. The modern histories of resistance to English dominance (in Ireland and the British Isles) and French dominance (in Brittany) contribute further to the myths unifying the Celtic fringe (see Map 1). Revival provides cultural glue that toughens the myths of Celtic unity.

The musicians who perform Celtic music and stage its revivals have skilfully determined the ways such factors of unity can be woven into music. Texts in Celtic languages obviously provide one of the ways in which music draws upon the store of unifying factors. Musical instruments, too, provide icons of unity for Celtic music. The instrument most commonly employed to represent the ancient qualities of Celtic music is the harp, the symbol of the great bardic traditions, whose singers are believed to have wandered throughout the Celtic lands singing epics in oral tradition. The instrumentarium for Celtic dance music, moreover, displays a high degree of unity, stretching from Scotland in the north to Galicia and Asturias in Spain, the southern extreme of Europe's Celtic fringe. In theory Celtic music should not be devoid of certain instrument types, for example bagpipes, which appear in local variants as different as Scotland's Highland pipes and Ireland's *uilleann* pipes. Attempts to integrate the musical traditions of Spanish Galicia have emphasized the survival of bagpipes in the north-western province of Spain.

Celtic music spreads across a geography linking Europe's Celtic fringe to the world, thereby transforming that geography into a landscape for world music. The geography of Celtic music-making is anchored by local sites, for example the Irish pub in which small

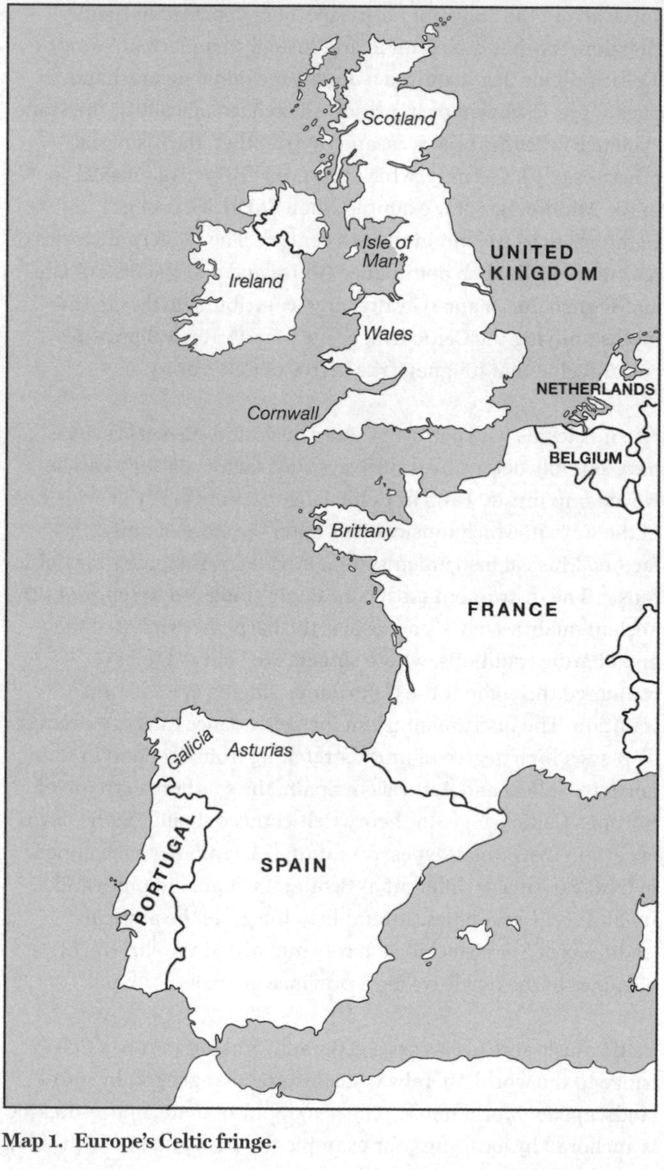

Map 1. Europe's Celtic fringe.

groups of musicians gather to perform in a so-called 'session'. Similarly, Irish folk dance thrives in cities like Chicago, with its long history of Irish immigration, in schools and competitions referred to as 'feis'. Connecting the local to the diasporic sites of music-making are many other forms of geography. The pilgrimage to Santiago de Compostela, Spain, one of the oldest of all Christian pilgrimages, has acquired Celtic significance as one of the largest cities of Galicia, metaphorically rerouting pilgrimages along the Celtic fringe to form postmodern confluences of Celtic religion and music.

There are no simple explanations for the remarkable transformation of Celtic music from folk music to world music. One might argue that there are numerous strands of tradition—mythic and historical—that form the synapses between the folk and world music elements. Their aesthetic stances on various repertories and styles notwithstanding, practitioners and fans of Celtic music would bridle at the suggestion that it was no longer folk music. Celtic music, so its defenders argue, has never lent itself to reduction to a single sound, style, or repertory, but rather has always accommodated change. The survival of Celtic undercurrents in North American bluegrass or country music serves as a witness to the resilience of folk music in diaspora. Fusion and revival have historically formed a counterpoint, with alternation between authenticity and experimentation coalescing around a centre that remains unequivocally Celtic. And forming the substance of that centre is folk music.

The Lomax family and American folk music scholarship

Just as there are genealogies of folk musicians, so too are there genealogies of folk music scholars. Whether one is modelled upon the other remains an open question, but there can be no question that the study of folk music accords high value to the transmission of music from one generation to the next, as well as laterally from one branch of a family to another. Genealogical metaphors fill the discourse characterizing oral tradition (e.g. the 'tune families' of Anglo-American folk song), and lineages of music scholars who have studied world music repertories that include folk music are surprisingly common—to name a few, Bruno Nettl and Stefan Fiol; Daniel M. Neuman and Dard Neuman; the author of this book and Andrea F. Bohlman. In the course of the 20th century two families of folk musicians and folk music scholars have played a particularly significant role in the collection and dissemination of American folk music—one with Charles Seeger (see Chapter 1) at its dynastic head, the other with John Lomax playing the foundational role—and it is to the Lomaxes that we turn briefly to understand the dynamics of genealogies.

John Avery Lomax (1867–1948), Alan Lomax (1915–2002), and Beth Lomax Hawes (1921–2009) all devoted their lives to folk music scholarship. Although Beth Lomax Hawes was a member of the well-known folk-revival group the Almanac Singers for over a decade (1941–52), the Lomax family largely approached folk music as scholars and popularists. If there is a theoretical common denominator shared by the entire family, it is that folk music belonged to those who made it but must be shared with a broader public. The Lomaxes were ideologically liberal, at times openly radical, and yet they never shied away from working with government agencies willing to support folk music. John Lomax became curator of the Archive of American Folk Song at the Library of Congress in 1933, and Beth Lomax Hawes was director of the Folk Arts Program of the National Endowment for the Arts from 1977 to 1992. Above all, the Lomaxes held that folk music was a resource, thus must be invested with the values of the national collective.

The publications of the Lomaxes provide a counterpoint to the history of the 20th century, beginning locally in the United States and expanding in increasingly global directions. The history of the numerous collections of and monographs on folk music begins in the American West, with John Lomax's pioneering study of cowboy songs, unfolds through volumes that give voice to African Americans and the downtrodden, and shifts to broader arenas that portend globalization theory. So expansive were the Lomax projects that several, especially the production of CDs from the Alan Lomax 'World Library of Folk and Primitive Music', continued into the 21st century. The influence of a century of folk music collecting has been vast. Lomax publications from the 1930s laid the groundwork for modern interpretations of the blues, and the great 'American' anthologies served as the canon for the folk revival in the 1950s.

Whether or not folk music really narrated history, locally, nationally, or internationally, was not a matter of debate for the Lomaxes. The power that folk music embodied was the power of strong wills, of 'hard hitting songs for hard-hit people' or ballads and songs that could be uplifted to America's very best. For the Lomaxes, it was out of the question that folk music would lose its power if repertories fell out of fashion. Folk music empowered one to seize the moment and to make a mark on history. One could hardly ask more of folk music than did John and Alan Lomax and Beth Lomax Hawes.

The Polka Belt—a place for folk music in the world

Can world music become folk music? Turning the question that opened the earlier section on Celtic music on its head seems almost banal in the 21st century. Even the most optimistic collectors and performers of folk music bemoan its decline and express concerns about endangerment. With the explosion and spread of world music it might seem that folk music, yet again, is about to fall victim to the very global forces to which it has so richly contributed.

Polka, however, tells a different story. The complexity of polka as a folk dance of international proportions blurs the distinctions between folk and world music and belies attempts to classify. Polka is found—and it thrives—just about anywhere in the world that Western music as folk, popular, and classical music has penetrated. With polka's original geographical epicentre in the northern part of today's Czech Republic, the dance spread across the Austro-Hungarian Empire and was passed on by emigrants, travelling musicians, and the salon music of European colonizers to the rest of the world. Wherever polka travelled, musicians domesticated the dance, adapting it to local social functions, ensemble structures, and aesthetic parameters. Wherever it was played, polka became local, again donning trappings as folk music. Once relocated and relocalized, polka's functions as folk music proliferated. It might assume a new identity through a new name, but it would win over new listeners and new dancers.

No single explanation accounts for polka's remarkable adaptability, for its insistence on reasserting folk qualities. Two general perspectives, however, prevail. We might regard the first perspective as top-down, a result of polka's inclusivity as a multiethnic, multicultural, and multigeneric music. According to this perspective, polka is not so much a style arising from a dance form—duple metre in ternary variants of ABA—as it is a sound aesthetic that stretches as an umbrella over musics expressing collective identity. In contrast, bottom-up perspectives focus on the centre of polka style, identifying certain traits that allow anyone and everyone to participate in performance, as musician, dancer, listener, or generally as aficionado. Polka is the music of the folk, and as such it expresses collective consciousness.

Both perspectives shed light on the geographical formation known as the 'Polka Belt', a cultural region defined by polka music stretching from the Dakotas of the USA and the prairie provinces of Canada to the ethnically diverse urban centres of the East (Map 2). The Polka Belt encompasses a region of considerable girth, where cultural and ethnic diversity is the norm. Musical styles move fluidly along the Polka Belt, from notch to notch, and they combine to express the unique character of polka at a given notch, for example the 'push style' developed in Chicago under

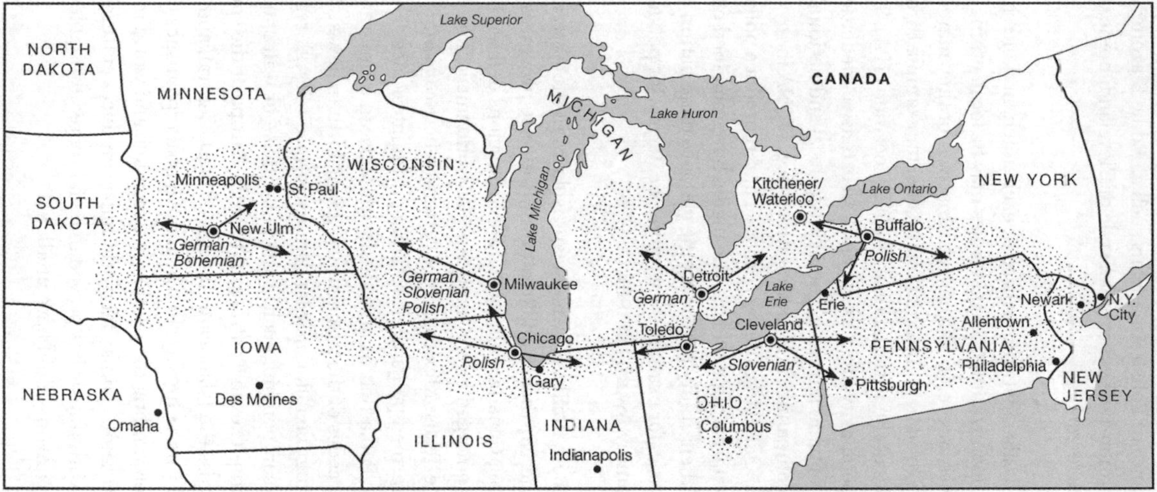

Map 2. The Polka Belt.

the dominance of Polish Americans such as Eddie Blazonczyk or the accordion-heavy Slovenian style of Cleveland, home to Frankie Yankovic.

Polka style is also institutionalized at each notch, in dance halls and social organizations. Social venues may be local, ethnic clubs and churches, or even polka clubs themselves, or they may connect the local to an international scene, for example through the activities of the International Polka Association (IPA). The historical popularity of polka depends on extensive mediation. Publishers of band parts and sheet music, local and national recording companies, and radio stations (e.g. WPNA in my own home town, Oak Park, Illinois) produce and reproduce polka music, disseminating it widely. The media have remained effective because of their ability to parallel the globalized mediation of popular music, for example by winning a category for polka in the annual Grammy Awards in 1986.

The Polka Belt, finally, is by no means isolated to the American Midwest and Northeast, and to ethnically diverse provinces in neighbouring Canada. Other geographical regions defined by polka have emerged on the landscapes of world music, for example the Texas–Mexico border regions, where *conjunto* fusions have transformed polka while retaining its quintessence. The cities of the Polka Belt have swelled with Mexican immigrants in the early decades of the 21st century, giving birth to new styles. By examining the folk music landscapes formed of local, regional, and global components, such as the Polka Belt—or waltz and *Ländler* complexes in Central and Eastern Europe or the spread of *ghazal*s across the Islamicate cultures of West, Central, and South Asia—we witness the ways in which the global replenishes the local. Understanding the relation between folk and world music asks us to rethink claims that world music produces cultural grey-out. World music has proved to be far more hospitable to folk music than anyone could have predicted.

Chapter 5
Music of the nations

In the name of the nation

Spring is one of the most intensive seasons of pilgrimage in Israel, with believers from each of the Abrahamic faiths (Judaism, Christianity, Islam) arriving from throughout the world to celebrate the confluence of spring pilgrimage festivals. In May 2019, another upsurge of pilgrims arrived in Israel, no less faithful, but searching not for healing or redemption as much as the celebration of national popular song at the 64th Eurovision Song Contest (ESC or simply Eurovision), which took place in Tel Aviv during 14–18 May. The ESC pilgrims dedicate themselves throughout the year to the competitions leading to the Grand Prix, which takes place in mid-May in the nation from which the previous year's winner came. The 2019 destination was Tel Aviv because the Israeli singer, Netta Barzilai, had captured 2018's top honours with her song, 'Toy'. The 2019 pilgrims would leave Tel Aviv planning already their journey to the Netherlands in 2020, whose entry, Duncan Lawrence, was victorious with 'Arcade'. The ESC pilgrims form various networks during the year, most of them with national bases, but many also distinctively international.

Eurovision networks stay connected in many different ways, materially and metaphorically. The ESC finds its home—with public and private financial support—in national broadcast networks (e.g. the BBC in the UK), each of which is a member of the largest broadcasting network worldwide, the European Broadcasting Union (EBU). It is the EBU and its major undertaking, the Eurovision, that connects the national to the international with events often far beyond Europe's borders. Israel is not in Europe, but it is a member-nation of the EBU. So too are Azerbaijan and Australia, annually since 2015 as a 'special guest' competing in the Eurovision.

Israel's hosting of the 2019 Eurovision once again sustained the symbolic national alliances with Europe, giving Israel a presence in international politics. Historically, Israel's participation might be said to have been more European than Israeli. Israel's earlier entries (e.g. Ofra Haza's second-place finish with 'Chai' [Alive] in 1983) bore witness to troubled moments in national history. It first competed in 1973, just after the assassination of Israeli athletes at the 1972 Munich Olympics and just before the 1973 Yom Kippur War. Through Eurovision participation Israel historically claimed musical territory beyond its national borders, especially those of religious law, for example as the first nation with a victorious trans* singer, Dana International, in 1998. In both the short and long term, the 64th ESC turned nations and nationalism inside-out, using world music to realign European politics in the world.

National and global histories have assumed many different forms for the ESC. The political history of the contest already marked its beginnings during a critical moment in the Cold War (the 1956 military incursion of the Soviet Union in Hungary and Czechoslovakia). ESC history provides a measure of the shift of European responses to international wars, post-colonial reconfiguration, the fall of communism, and the expansion of the European Union. Local and regional histories, as well as the *longue durée* of struggles over empire and nation-state within Europe, shape Eurovision songs, reflecting the globalization of popular world music. So intertwined are these multiple histories that the ESC is referred to by Eurovision scholar, Dafni Tragaki, as an 'empire of song'.

There is a confounding paradox that accompanies the competition at the heart of the Eurovision: each nation must represent its own national identity and the traits that make it different and distinctive, while at the same time sounding the common culture of Europe. The structure of each song and performance makes this paradox even more vexing, for a Eurovision song must conform to the following restrictions:

- song duration must be exactly three minutes
- there may be no more than six performers on the stage at any moment
- vocalists, both soloists and backup singers, perform live
- instrumentalists do not perform live, but rather mimic performance over recorded sound
- specific political gestures are not allowed

The aesthetic and musical questions that must be answered to resolve the paradox of representing a nation transnationally are themselves vexing. Does one sing in a language all will understand, or in the language of one's own nation, even when understood by relatively few Europeans (e.g. Latvian or Romanian)? What if there are multiple languages for a nation (e.g. Belgium and Spain)? Is a national song or dance form too folksy or unintelligible, or is it possible to transform transnational genres into national forms? The answers to such questions must resolve the tension between the national and the nationalist. Paradoxically, the formal constraints and internal repetition in Eurovision song style can be, and often are, primary sources of creativity. Creativity resides in the ways tightly formalized songs allow for national differences.

Critical to the ways popular-song form represents a nation in the three minutes allotted a Eurovision song are the many ways in which the middle section—the 'bridge'—becomes a site of difference. The middle section shifts temporal registers to become the site of the political, potentially performing a call for nationalist action and protest. In '1944', Ukraine's winning song in 2016, it is in the bridge that Jamala switches from English to Crimean Tatar, thus making the reference to Russian annexation of Ukraine explicit (see below). When engendering national fantasy, individual Eurovision songs move from the non-representational to the highly symbolic, negotiating the borders between the national and the nationalist year after year.

Good nationalism, bad nationalism

Throughout its long history nationalism has taken many different forms—political nationalism, religious nationalism, linguistic nationalism, ethnic nationalism—all of which together overlap and intersect. At some historical moments, for example, when a nation achieves independence from a colonial power, nationalism contains much that is positive about a nation. At other moments, for example, in the second decade of the 21st century, when conflict and violence throughout the world have led to a global refugee crisis, nationalism has emerged as a counterforce capturing a nation's most negative attributes. Through its two forms—the positive and the negative—nationalism asserts its basic power either to unite or to divide. In its positive forms nationalism inspires many to embrace globalization, placing a high value on a larger community of nations. In its negative forms nationalism feeds on the fear of others, especially coming from outside the nation, unleashing actions of exceptionalism and isolationalism. Nationalism may be founded on universal values, such as the struggle for human rights globally. It may also be rooted in the soils of prejudice and racism, as in the rise of white nationalism in the 21st century.

There may well be no more common symbol for world music than the nation. The parsing of world music as national music is as old as the nation itself; or perhaps as old as nationalism itself. When

Johann Gottfried Herder (see Chapter 2) first forged a vocabulary describing world music, he drew upon national concepts. When publishing his volumes of *Volkslieder*, or 'Folk Songs', he provided an attribution of nation and language to accompany the song's title: the first two songs in his seminal anthology were 'German' and 'English', the final song 'Peruvian'. Herder's vocabulary was critical because it established a process of inscribing world music, transforming it from an oral phenomenon to a national language. The processes of inscribing world music may have become more technologically elaborate in the 21st century, but they continue to privilege the nation on the map of world music. When musicological and ethnomusicological reference works at the beginning of the 21st century—say, the ten-volume *Garland Encyclopedia of World Music* or the most comprehensive of all music reference works worldwide, *Grove Music Online*—expand the surveying tools for world music, they may add conceptual categories, but they do not abandon the nation.

The nation is an ontological fact of life in the study of world music. Positively or negatively construed, nationalism enhances the exclusivity of national music. Rather than representing the nation as a whole with benefits for every citizen, nationalist music can acquire more specific functions, perhaps the dissemination of a restrictive set of ideological values or the aggrandizement of a ruling ethnic group. Music presents the nation with a way of preserving its past and thus writing the history of its present. We witness acts of preserving the nation in the designations by Japan and South Korea of musicians who are 'national treasures', whose performance thus prevents national musical traditions from disappearing. National musics rendered as nationalist musics may lead a nation to war or claim land that belongs to someone else. The rise of right-wing political parties worldwide during the 21st century has been sounded by new and old repertories of nationalist song. In order to bolster its insistence on Hinduism at the confluence of political and religious nationalism in India, the conservative Hindutva movement has called for more extensive teaching of the Sanskrit epics, *Rāmāyaṇa* and *Mahābhārata*, as contingent narratives in India's history. By injecting nationalist sentiments into national music collections, scholars and government agencies alike *ipso facto* make room for some citizens while taking away space from others.

Music, because of its performativity, can powerfully shape the nation. To explain this performative power of music Benedict Anderson has applied the term 'unisonance', the sonic moment that occurs when people from throughout the nation gather in a shared performance of music. The unisonant moment may occur when a national anthem is being sung. We might add to Anderson's nationalist examples the broadcast of Eurovision entries over state broadcasting networks, which have the effect of encouraging all citizens occupying a public national soundscape to listen communally. Unisonance can also produce a site of silence and resistance, notably at athletic events in the United States, when athletes and fans protest the forms of injustice enunciated by the 'Black Lives Matter' movement by refusing to sing the 'Star Spangled Banner'.

When the nation joins together as a singing nation, the communal experience of music-making generates a feeling of cultural intimacy, what Michael Herzfeld calls the 'social poetics' of the nation-state. Significantly, it is not one genre or repertory of music (e.g. folk music) that lends itself to cultural intimacy, but virtually all kinds: popular, religious, and classical music, vocal and instrumental music, revered historical repertories and the latest hit songs. When the nation joins in the performance of musical styles it deems its own, it effectively breaks down the barriers between repertories that otherwise might have made them exclusive. For these reasons, folk song finds its way into symphonic poems, and sacred songs become national anthems. The music of the nation mirrors the two sides of nationalism, producing two contrasting sets of traits. The musical traits that reinforce a nation's internal image of selfness often fall under the rubric of the 'national in music'. Those traits expressing how one nation distinguishes itself from others are called, in contrast, the 'nationalist in music'. We might summarize these different ways of singing the nation as in Box 5.

The Eurovision singer as the voice of *Realpolitik* in real-time

On 13 April 2017, Yulia Samoylova, the Russian entry in the 2017 Eurovision Song Contest, received notice from the European Broadcasting Union that she would not be able to compete in the finals of the ESC, only a month away in Kyiv, Ukraine. Russia's expulsion from the 2017 Eurovision followed weeks of controversy during which Samoylova was informed she would be denied

Box 5 National music and nationalist music

The national in music	The nationalist in music
National culture is generated from within	Nationalist culture is threatened from without
Folk song is a national treasure	Art song elevates the nation's image
Metaphors drawn from nature	Metaphors stress modern advances
National myth precedes history	History grows from myth
The national language is distinctive and unique	The national language is cosmopolitan
Extensive use of dialect	Written forms of language in lyrics
Oral tradition generates written tradition	Written tradition enhances oral tradition
Musical practice is local and individual	Musicians are mobile and collective

entry into Ukraine because she had previously performed in Russian-annexed Crimea without a Ukrainian visa. From Ukraine's point of view Samoylova had entered Ukraine illegally, her performance an act of supporting Russia's 2014 seizure of Crimea. The EBU attempted to resolve what increasingly appeared as a political impasse between two of the most prominent and successful Eurovision competitors, Russia and Ukraine. Russia had the option of sending a different entry, or, alternatively, Samoylova could compete virtually, that is, live for television in Moscow but broadcast simultaneously to Kyiv. Defiantly, Russian Channel 1 decided instead to withdraw from the 2017 ESC and not to broadcast the two semi-final competitions (9 and 11 May 2017) or the Grand Finale (13 May 2017). The political, economic, and military conflict between Ukraine and Russia had entered real-time, the international performance of popular music.

Time, historical and in the present, was critical to how nationalism proliferated in the real-time of the 2017 Eurovision. The 2016 Ukrainian entry, Jamala (Susana Alimivna Jamaladinova; b. 1983), a well-known singer of Crimean-Tatar heritage, had sharpened the historical focus on political narrative with her winning song '1944', combining song text and performance context from past and present. The '1944' in the title textually referred to the Soviet purge and deportation of Crimean-Tatars during the Second World War. The references to the Russian annexation of Crimea in 2014, nonetheless, were lost on no one when the Tatar refrain (here shown in translation) switched to first-person voice that collapsed past and present:

> I did not enjoy my youth. I was unable to live in this place. I did not enjoy my youth.
> I was unable to live in this place.

Jamala's '1944' was the victorious song in the Eurovision Song Contest sixty years after the inaugural Europe-wide competition for national popular song, the Grand Prix Eurovision de la

Chanson Européenne, on 24 May 1956 in Lugano, Switzerland. The symbols of temporality and history abounded also in the first competition, won by Switzerland's Lys Assia (1924–2018), who performed the song, 'Refrain':

Refrain, couleur du ciel,	Let us see you once more, colour of the sky,
Parfum de mes vingt ans	The fragrance I knew when only twenty,
Jardin plein de soleil	The sun graces the garden
Où je courais enfant.	Through which a small child was running.

The circumstances connecting '1944' and 'Refrain' and the moments of their Eurovision performances, at the beginning of Eurovision history in 1956 and in the real-time juxtaposed in 2016/17, are uncannily similar. In 1956, Europe stood at one of the most critical moments during the Cold War, when the Soviet army occupied Hungary and Czechoslovakia, situating them in communist Eastern Europe for another three and a half decades. In 2016, Russian seizure of Ukrainian territory would militarize what was increasingly recognized as a new Cold War. Their historical similarities notwithstanding, the Eurovisions of 1956 and 2016 seem like two entirely different musical moments. It is the similarity and difference of these moments on the most globally mediated of all musical stages in the world that affords them power to narrate national histories in the real-time realized through the transgression of national borders.

National anthems

At one of the deepest levels of our popular-culture subconscious we all share a common image of national anthems: the victory ceremonies at the quadrennial Olympic Games. There, on platforms in full view of the international media, stand the victors, struggling to hold back tears and to mouth the words of their national anthems. It is a moment of national pride framed by music. The moments are often memorable; the national anthems are often less so. Is anyone really listening? Does anyone really care? To answer these questions I turn to one of the most ubiquitous of all types of world music, the national anthem. In the history of nation-building, there have been many who have cared a great deal about national anthems. Many anthems have enjoyed long histories; many nations have inscribed their histories in amazingly complex ways by selecting and discarding, revising and recomposing, their national anthems. National anthems are serious business, and it is for that reason they are performed at the most solemn moments dedicated to performing a nation's essence.

When we hear national anthems, not to mention when we really listen to them, we are nonetheless struck by a paradox: do they not all sound rather alike? At public moments of patriotic pride, when national identity is at issue, we might expect some striking differences. The most recently created national anthems for the post-colonial nations of Africa and Asia, however, do not sound ostensibly different from the anthems of previous colonizers. To confuse the matter even more, there are the anthems of different nations that are, in fact, the same, or have the same composer and lyricist, the case of the national anthems of India and Bangladesh, both created by Rabindranath Tagore (1861–1941), who died before either achieved national independence, India in 1947, Bangladesh in 1971.

If one traces the histories of national anthems, it is clear that many came into existence when rupture and crisis were motivations for their creation. When Rhodesia proclaimed independence from Great Britain in 1965, it discarded 'God Save the Queen' and detoured briefly through the international territory of the Beethoven/Schiller 'Ode to Joy', before Zimbabwe, almost three decades after independence, adopted an anthem with the Shona title, 'Simudzai mureza wedu weZimbabwe' (Lift high Zimbabwe's banner) in 1994. There are both textual and contextual reasons that national anthems may sound alike. First of all, many new anthems are based on previously existing anthems. The most common models have been the United Kingdom's 'God Save the Queen', France's 'La Marseillaise', and Franz Joseph Haydn's 'Kaiserhymne'. International anthems (see the final section of this chapter), too, have served as models for national anthems, notably the 'Internationale' and final movement of Beethoven's Ninth Symphony. Second, though the anthems are of distinct genres (e.g. hymns or marches), performance practice tends to create homogeneity. Finally, anthems may sound alike because they are played at occasions more alike than different, for example at state ceremonies or athletic events, in the theatre or cinema, or to punctuate national radio and television broadcasts.

The history of national anthems parallels that of nationalism, unfolding through a series of historiographical stages, beginning with the Enlightenment in the 18th century, Romantic nationalism (especially in Europe and Latin America) in the 19th century, colonial expansion from the late 19th century until the Second World War, and post-colonialism from the mid-20th century to the present. At each of these stages the national anthem meant something different. Typically, the earliest national anthems captured some of the sound and function of folk songs. In the middle stages, national songs aspired to religious and military genres. During the post-colonial stage, national anthems characteristically attempted to embody a modern nation's history.

National anthems appeared in two different ways, which together are suggestive of the multiple meanings that converge when a nation is given voice through song. The first of these ways would seem on its surface to be most familiar to us: a nation decides to proclaim its nationhood through song, and it sets a composer, or, not uncommonly, a lyricist to the task. The other way in which national songs come into existence might be compared to the use of a massive vacuum cleaner that is shoved in the direction of everything imagined to fulfil some characteristic of the national. We notice this approach because it often begins by producing anthologies whose songs collectively represent the nation. In such anthologies, 'our' national melodies often mingle with 'theirs', locking self and other in mutual style demarcation. Such a process was set in motion by an American collecting project that would lead to the first internationally comprehensive publication of national anthems, a volume edited by US Marine Corps Bandmaster John Philip Sousa for the US Navy Department, *National, Patriotic and Typical Airs of All Lands* (1890). We might marvel at such a project, and expect that its fulfilment as a 'Special Order' from the Secretary of the Navy would lead to a superficial potpourri of melodies, but in fact the 283-page volume is executed with meticulous detail and carefully crafted harmonizations and arrangements, all accompanied by copious footnotes and ethnographic information. The final six pages, for example, contain national songs from Wales, Wallachia, Yap Island, Zamboanga Island, and Zanzibar, sources that might not easily find their way into modern anthologies of national song.

There is nothing simple about national anthems, and to illustrate precisely this point let me briefly sketch the very equivocal biography of the most unequivocally charged of all modern national anthems, known as the 'Deutschlandlied', or 'Germany-Song', but called by German- and non-German-speakers alike, 'Deutschland, Deutschland über alles' (Germany, Germany, above all else). The anthem's melody, called the 'Kaiserhymne' (Emperor's hymn), first served as the source for the anthem of the Austro-Hungarian Empire. The 'Emperor's Hymn' was composed as a set of variations for a string quartet (Hob. III:77) in 1797 by Franz Joseph Haydn. The melody derives from a Croatian folk song, variants of which today survive in the Croatian parts of the Austrian province of Burgenland, one of the most intensively multicultural regions of Central Europe. The next major chapter in the song's biography begins in 1841, when August Heinrich Hoffmann von Fallersleben, a school teacher from Silesia (today in south-western Poland), wrote the poem 'Deutschland, Deutschland über alles', while in political exile on the North Sea island of Heligoland, at that time held by England. Whether or not the German national anthem is today world music is not the question, but rather how its journeys, as one of the most identifiable and oft-copied national anthems, entered a history of world music articulated clearly and contentiously by national anthems.

Music scholarship without borders

The paradox of representation we trace through this chapter—how to be at once international and respectful of national approaches to music—also accompanies the global agenda of the two major international societies of music scholarship, the International Council for Traditional Music (ICTM) and the International Musicological Society (IMS). The call for musical scholarship whose goals would extend beyond national differences—the 'Preface' to the 2017 *History of the IMS* begins with the motto, 'musicologists without borders'—has been explicit since their foundational years. In both cases, political and ideological necessity enforced the paradox. In its early years the IMS responded to the rise of fascism in Central Europe, long the centre of music scholarship. The ICTM, originally called the International Council for Folk Music, came into being a generation and a global conflagration later, during the division of the world through the Cold War. The frequent claims by both societies that their members work beyond borders have always been hopeful and tentative, for nations, even as they support research into the universal dimensions of music, far more commonly leave tolerance and understanding on the more familiar sides of international borders.

The ICTM has historically regarded its name with no less ambiguity than its 'official' object of study: 'to assist in the study, practice, documentation, preservation and dissemination of traditional music, including folk, popular, classical and urban and dance, of all countries'. Calling itself the International Folk Music Council (IFMC) when founded in 1947, the IFMC renamed itself as the ICTM in 1981, dismantling the boundaries of what many members regarded as Eurocentric disciplinary practices. However sweeping such conceptual reorganization was, it left the political organization of the ICTM intact. The broadly defined musical object—stretching from folk to classical to urban—necessarily found itself in 'all countries'. At the core of the ICTM's cultural politics has been the nation with its institutional form of 'national committees'. ICTM international politics take place at the borders between nations, above all through affiliation with organizations such as the International Music Council and UNESCO. However an individual member chooses to study world music, the ICTM locates it in the nation, or rather 'all countries'.

Founded in 1927, the IMS has struggled to define its international reach in quite different ways. Building on the heritage of Austro-German historical musicology, the IMS was shaped by approaches to music placing it within the provenance of European civilization. Musics outside the European art music tradition were not excluded per se, but they posed an ontological problem of otherness. National differences remained very much intact, for example, through the membership of committees and governing boards, and, strikingly, in the publication of research in five official languages in the IMS journal, *Acta Musicologica* (of which, I should confess here, I have been co-editor since 2011). Neither the ICTM nor the IMS rests easily with the national/international paradox they have historically confronted, but rather they call for continued awareness of how the paradox has proved divisive in the history of world music.

Beyond the nation—super-, supra-, and international anthems

For aesthetic, ontological, and political reasons national music rests uneasily at the borders of the nation. National music complicates the relation between the nation and world music, giving way to the super- and supranational conditions of nationalism, and to the creation of genres that we might call 'international anthems'. International anthems exist in a complex counterpoint with national songs. There are times when they bolster each other, in moments such as the Olympic Games, when the 'Olympic Anthem' (composed by Spiro Samara in 1896) represents a global community of nations, while national anthems represent the constituent members of the community. National and international anthems are not the same, but one depends on the other. Songs usually do not become international anthems overnight. Melodies may or may not contain characteristics that reflect an international character. On one hand, some of the most widely used international anthems have rather complex melodic structures that make them difficult to sing; this is true of the 'Internationale', which requires a wide melodic range from the singer. On the other hand, international anthems are, with very few exceptions, choral works, requiring concerted performance by a mass of individuals whose cultural differences may be extreme.

Specific historical moments usually engender the chain of events that shape and reshape an international song. An anthem itself may or may not directly participate in such moments. In the case of the 'Internationale' the song and the events are virtually inseparable. The text of the 'Internationale' issued from the pen of Eugène Pottier, who wrote the poem in 1871 during the French suppression of the Paris Commune. The melody and original setting of the song were the work of Pierre Degeyter, a textile worker and choral director from Lille, who, legend has it, unearthed a collection of Pottier's 'revolutionary songs'. For the worldwide socialist movement, the pedigrees of worker and musician were extremely important, in effect meaning that the song could mobilize the very struggle from which it was born. The history of the 'Internationale' was indeed international from the outset. Labour unions adopted it, as did socialist organizations of all kinds. It symbolized the struggle of the voiceless, and it quickly gave them voice by undergoing countless translations and settings (Box 6).

Box 6 L'Internationale/The Internationale

Lyrics: Eugène Pottier; Music: Pierre Degeyter

Debout, les damnés de la terre,	Arise, the wretched of the earth,
Debout, les forçats de la faim.	Arise, those in the bonds of starvation.
La raison tonne en son cratère,	Reason issues forth like a volcano,
C'est l'éruption de la fin.	Its eruption no longer contained.
Du passé faisons table rase,	We must make the past a tabula rasa,
Foule esclave, debout, debout.	The many who are slaves, arise, arise.
Le monde va changer de base,	The world will now forever change,
Nous ne sommes rien, soyons tout.	No more are we nothing as we now embrace all.
Chorus	
C'est la lutte finale,	Our struggle now comes to its end,
Groupons-nous, et demain	As we draw our forces together so that tomorrow
L'Internationale sera le genre humain.	The Internationale will join all people as one.

The world united by the 'Internationale' was a loose ideological and political confederacy. There have been many international songs whose lives began on the level of loose confederacy, but have followed an increasingly narrow path toward nationalism. This was the case with 'HaTikva' (Hope), which channelled several musical and textual streams on its way from a song in the international Zionist movement to Israeli national anthem. Already at the first Zionist Congresses in the late 19th century, 'HaTikva' had found its way to the cultural stage of an international Jewish organization that was still relatively inchoate. The song changed all that, for by encouraging the delegates to join together in song—as a body of choristers from throughout the world—the early Zionists created a common voice. The song was first forged as a single song in 1886 by Naphtali Herz Imber (1856–1909). When 'HaTikva' became a national anthem for Israel, that too was a natural result of its symbolic power, affording the shift from international to national, paralleling the ingathering of immigrants from throughout the world.

Forging international anthems has become a preoccupation of many attempting to create policies of regional and global unification at the turn of our own century. As with previous attempts to map the nation onto the world while obscuring the nation's borders, the synthesis of postmodern international songs requires a fusion of myth and history: tales about European anthems weave together fact and historical imagination. The European Union does not have an official cultural policy, but rather an official hands-off policy, stated as Article 128 of the 'Treaty on European Union' thus: 'The Community shall contribute to the flowering of the cultures of the Member States, while respecting their national and regional diversity and at the same time bringing the common cultural heritage to the fore.' There had previously been suggestions about using the 'Ode to Joy', Beethoven's setting in his Ninth Symphony of Friedrich Schiller's Enlightenment paean to universal brotherhood, as an anthem for the United Nations. Already in 1972, Herbert von

Karajan had undertaken an arrangement of the 'Ode to Joy' for the Committee of Ministers of the Council of Europe, but at that time it found little consensus, not least because of Karajan's previous participation in Nazi cultural activities. Stylistic questions also arose, for example about the real nature of Beethoven's international style in the final movement of the Ninth Symphony, also notable for its orientalist style, not least the insertion of a Turkish march in a middle section.

The question remains, then, Whose nations and whose world might international anthems unify? Will the political ends of national music be inclusive or exclusive, for example, as new nations join the EU and others, such as the United Kingdom in the wake of its 2020 Brexit departure from the European Union, seek to leave? The Beethoven/Schiller 'Ode to Joy' does not answer those questions, but it certainly poses them. National music and nationalism in music have historically been extremely public phenomena, for they seize the stage of history, perhaps in choral movements mobilizing political movements, perhaps in battles between colonizer and colonized. The stakes for claiming the stage of a nation with music are very high indeed.

Chapter 6
Diaspora

Diasporic re-encounters, 1492–1992

1492 was a year that proved to unleash diaspora upon diaspora. It was in 1492 that Columbus 'discovered' the New World, which soon thereafter became a colonial space virtually defined by its alterity, the fact that it was not the Old World. With the New World opened for colonization, new possibilities for settlement were set in motion, some advantageous for the Old World—establishing new trade networks or escaping religious persecution—most disadvantageous for just about everyone from other 'worlds' that did not enjoy the historical privileges gained by Europe. In 1492, the *reconquista*—the retaking of the Iberian Peninsula from the non-Europeans and non-Christians who had lived there for centuries—also came to a dramatic conclusion when all Muslims and Jews were forcibly driven from Spain. In the century after 1492 human displacement was massive and worldwide, plotting what Timothy Rommen has called 'landscapes of diaspora' as a defining condition of early modernism.

During the centuries of the early modern and the modern eras, the '92s', those years that mark the passing of another century since Spain's historic unleashing of diaspora, have generated considerable celebration. The 92s witness world fairs, for example, which assemble cultures from throughout the world and put them on display. The cultural endeavours of the years leading up to the 92s are global in proportion, if for no other reason than the almost banal fact that 1492 was the first consciously historical moment of global history. The music mustered to mark and celebrate a 92 celebration is, by extension, world music. At the 1893 World's Columbian Exposition in Chicago (so massive was the fair that organizers were a year late in opening its doors) there were countless performances of world music, and at least 103 of these appeared on the first systematic recordings of world music at the fair (see Chapter 7). In 1892 (or 1893) there was little discussion of diaspora per se, but much recognition of the world dominance the West had maintained in the centuries following 1492.

In 1992 the celebrations were again vocal and global. The New World threw itself a birthday party, and in the Old World Spain, especially, missed few opportunities to announce the global role it had played 500 years earlier. At the 1992 anniversary questions of displacement and diaspora were addressed more critically. It was in 1992 that more critical judgement on the expulsion of Jews was passed. The designation of the expelled Jews, 'Sephardic', found a new currency, even though few realized that the Hebrew *Sepharad* translates as 'Spain'. Sephardic culture was diasporic and global, all the more so because it formed from a previous diaspora, necessitated by the destruction of the Temple in Jerusalem in 70 CE. In the historiography of the Jewish diaspora, the Sephardic diaspora within a diaspora had remained relatively unknown as a chapter in the history of modern Israel. All that changed in 1992 when Sephardic history took its place as one of the ways of re-encountering 1492. This act of revisionist historiography happened almost overnight as Sephardic music transformed the past into a diasporic present. Sephardic music had survived because it was portable. Sephardic folk music, especially, was narrative, with genres such as the *romance* weaving historical accounts into the stories of ballads. For Sephardic music, 1992 marked the moment of transition to world music.

The Sephardic diaspora was hardly the first to possess the potential dimensions of world music. The term 'diaspora' had a long currency, originally referring to the dispersion of classical Greek civilization from the central city-states to the peripheral islands and colonies. Jewish history, too, was interpreted from Jewish and non-Jewish perspectives as diasporic. 1992, nonetheless, marked a watershed, for almost without anyone's noticing it, many different cultures and human displacements had acquired the characteristics—and name—of a diaspora. There were, for example, African, Irish, and South Asian diasporas, whose musics, too, inscribed the boundaries and routes of diaspora. Diaspora became a musical context for encounter, migration, and fusion.

The diasporas of the 1990s reflected the historicism of 1992 and previous 92s in different but distinctive ways. In the present chapter both historical and modern diasporas—the Jewish, African, South Asian, and Indian Ocean diasporas—will serve as leitmotifs, each historicizing different moments of the encounter formed by modernity and globalization. These diasporas bear witness to the political, historical, and musical conditions of modernity. In the 21st century denying a culture, displaced or not, the status of a diaspora on some level has also denied it a place in a global culture. In the 21st century diaspora itself offers a place where world music takes place, nurturing and emphasizing its very placelessness.

Place and placelessness in world music

As a condition of placelessness, diaspora has become one of the places most articulated by world music. The music of diaspora is about places of being and places of becoming, of connecting the present with its absence of place to the past and the future. The process of imagining a sense of place to supplant placelessness necessarily produces hybridity formed from juxtaposing repertories gathered during histories of global journey. Diaspora assumes very diverse forms, but it is possible to describe three general conditions that force people from a place regarded as their own. First, there are religious reasons leading to expulsion from a sacred homeland. The journey from that place of origin assumes sacred dimensions, above all because providence requires a journey of return. Some of the historically oldest diasporas, notably the Jewish diaspora, have become profoundly sacred precisely because of the promise of return. Second, there are peoples and cultures with no place to call their own, thus making it necessary to move ceaselessly. Again, there are classic cases of such diasporas, those of Roma and Sinti peoples being very well known. Third, there are more modern diasporas spawned by conflict and economic struggle. The widespread migrations following from the breakup of empires and civil war are among the chief causes for the third type of diaspora.

Drawing upon W. E. B. Du Bois's notion of African American double consciousness, Paul Gilroy has suggestively theorized the 'Black Atlantic' as a conceptual space in which cultural traits with both African and non-African origins interact. Double, or sometimes multiple, consciousnesses make it possible for groups to maintain cultural practices that express connectedness to a historical homeland while adapting to new homelands. The musics of Du Bois's 'Afro-America' or Gilroy's 'Black Atlantic' thus can differ radically from each other, yet share certain common traits. Music, as Gilroy and other theorists of multiple consciousness have been quick to demonstrate, emerges as one of the most powerfully symbolic forms of common tradition, affording the means of negotiating with outside cultures in the diasporic environment.

Musical instruments often serve as some of the most palpable traces of origin in diaspora. In the African diaspora musical instruments accompanied slaves freighted across the Middle Passage, and the memory of instrumental practices and ensembles was revived across the Americas as slaves and former slaves employed music to remember the ancestral past. Xylophone-type instruments, with wooden and metal slabs, have long served as evidence for the retention of instruments from West African ensembles. Xylophone-type instruments, furthermore, have provided empirical evidence for connecting African concepts of rhythm and time to African American and Afro-Caribbean musics. In East and South-East Asia, other instruments have played important roles in the inscription of diaspora. The metallophone orchestras of South-East Asia (e.g. the Javanese gamelan) reflect diasporic patterns that bear witness to multiple linguistic and musical connections.

The diasporic patterns of musical instruments are not simply a matter of dispersion and dissemination. Exchange across the borders between multiple consciousnesses is often even more significant. The instrumentarium of the South Asian diaspora has historically played a significant role in the crossing of religious, linguistic, and social borders in South Asia. With the colonial era, entirely new and seemingly foreign instruments were imported to India. The violin and clarinet found their ways into Karnatak (South Indian) classical music, while the harmonium established itself in the light classical and devotional music of Hindustani (North Indian) music. Sitars (long-necked plucked lutes) and tablas (a set of two small drums) from Hindustani music found their way quickly into Western jazz and rock 'n' roll (we need but remember George Harrison in *Norwegian Wood*) and the South Asian fusion genres that abound in Bollywood films. The harmonium, its Western origins notwithstanding, now charts the South Asian diaspora, so much so that the world centre for harmonium manufacture is Kolkata.

Throughout this chapter we witness the ways in which the explosion in world music is paralleled by the proliferation of diaspora. When we ask why this is, we find ourselves greeted by quite complex answers, many of them rather disturbing. First, there are more groups who consciously give unity to otherwise barely related patterns of immigration by remapping them as diasporas. Ethnic Irish abroad, for example, increasingly refer to themselves as an Irish diaspora. Some of the new diasporas may well be inventions, for example the Celtic diaspora, but they nonetheless bespeak a deep concern about multiple consciousness. World music offers a musical place for the narratives of diaspora, be they national or religious, or responses to the violation of human rights. This has surely proved to be the case with the Muslim diaspora in Central Europe, the South Asian diaspora in the UK, and the North African diaspora in Spain and France. For many stateless peoples, for example the Kurds, whose homeland straddles the borders of Turkey, Syria, Iraq, and Iran, world music has temporarily transformed the placelessness of diaspora into a place for expressing common history.

Bob Marley—weaving the diasporic web

Diaspora unfolded like concentric rings throughout Bob Marley's career. Marley (1945–81), at the centre of diasporic rings, consciously wove together the global mix of musical styles that intersected in the Caribbean. His diasporic musical web drew its strands from musical, historical, ideological, and religious sources, connecting Jamaica and the Caribbean to Africa and Europe, confronting the encounters of colonizer and colonized, slave master and slave. Marley's mixtures of ska and reggae, his impact on rock and rap alike, his evocations of Rastafarianism and resistance, might well have collapsed under the weight of their own eclecticism had he not discovered a common theme to bind them together: diaspora.

Bob Marley's life itself acquired the dimensions of a sacred journey. The stations of his short life were many, each one drawing upon the complex histories that intersected in his personal life and in the public arena of Jamaican music. The son of a black mother from rural Jamaica and a mixed-blood father from the urban administrative class, Marley absorbed a particularly

Jamaican form of double consciousness. His formative years were spent in rural Jamaica, but in his early teens he moved to Kingston. By the age of 18, he had formed the core of his band, the Wailers. Already before the production of his first ska album in 1965, he had released several hit songs, among them 'Judge Not' and 'Put It Down'. The broad outlines of Marley's life are relatively well known. Instrumentalists entered and exited from the Wailers, but the configuration known as Bob Marley and the Wailers remained more or less intact from the 1970s, when they made a series of groundbreaking albums: *Rastaman Vibration* (1976), *Survival* (1979), *Zimbabwe* (1979), and *Uprising* (1980). After a long struggle with cancer Marley died in 1981, leaving a legacy of songs expressing the many dimensions of diaspora and lasting hits such as 'I Shot the Sheriff' and 'Redemption Song'.

Bob Marley came to symbolize the double consciousness of diaspora by making several different kinds of connections to Africa and underscoring the commonality of Jamaicans and Africans. Marley also turned to the religious domain of diaspora, notably in his intense involvement with Rastafarianism, the symbols of which formed a metaphorical path of a return to the Africa of the earliest black Christians. The musical path for that return moved from metaphorical to real in the stylistic changes heralded by Marley's music, from the reworking of African *akete* drums in the rhythm of ska in the early 1960s to the integrative Africanness of rock steady in the late 1960s to the full articulation of a Jamaicanized Rastafarianism in reggae by the early 1970s. His was a musical career that recharted the journey of Jamaican popular music, mapping reggae as a music of diaspora.

Music's place in the South Asian diaspora

Tales of music abound in the vast body of South Asian literature. One of the major figures of that literary tradition, Amit Chaudhuri (b. 1962), enjoys international careers as both a musician and a writer. Among his most musical works is the novel, *Afternoon*

Raag, the story of a Bengali student at Oxford, whose own relation to England unfolds as a brilliantly mirrored series of vignettes. The narrative thread that binds the vignettes as snapshots constituting a *Bildungsroman* is music. Interspersed among the encounters with friends and lovers are the accounts of music lessons at the home of the narrator's teacher, a brother of his guru in India. The narratives of *rāga*—the Hindustani system of melodic modes signalled in the novel's title—are laden with journeys that draw the narrator closer to India through each rehearsal of the *rāg*s appropriate to the afternoon hours when the lessons take place. For the narrator of the novel to experience the *rāg* in his lessons is also to return home.

Properly speaking, the dispersion of South Asians has produced not one, but many diasporas. The diasporas bear witness to a multitude of origins: indentured servitude in the 19th century, particularly responsible for the Indian populations in the Caribbean and the British colonies of eastern and southern Africa; the political implosion of the subcontinent in the mid-20th century; the emigration of Pakistanis and Bengalis in search of economic opportunities elsewhere; the exportation of Indian workers to the Gulf States in the 21st century; the refugee crisis faced by Rohingyas along the borders of Myanmar and Bangladesh. The South Asian diaspora has a literature of its own, with authors such as Chaudhuri, V. S. Naipaul, and Salman Rushdie serving as avuncular figures for a younger generation. The maturity of the self-reflection such writers weave into their fiction has exerted a profound effect on South Asia, where the language of the diaspora, English, has become the primary language of the literary homeland.

South Asian music also has a mature presence in the diaspora. Many Indian musicians spend as much time abroad as at home, not just performing but also teaching. For children born in the diaspora, especially in the urban and academic centres that serve as nodes in the diaspora's web, it is not particularly difficult to learn traditional Indian music or study the classical-dance forms, such as *bharatanātyam* and *kathak*. The LPs of an older generation of South Asian musicians, of Ravi Shankar and Ali Akbar Khan, are familiar throughout the West, but so too are the CDs and YouTube performances of a younger generation that has lived almost entirely in the West, for example the tabla virtuoso, Zakir Hussain, and the rapper, M.I.A. The musical maturity of the South Asian diaspora is possible because music has mapped it on so many different places in the diaspora. It is to a brief description of some of those places that we now turn.

Point of origin and return. At first glance, it may seem paradoxical that musics of the South Asian diaspora identify points of origin as specifically as possible, rather than simply referring generally to India, Pakistan, Bangladesh, Nepal, or Sri Lanka. Bhangra (see Box 7), no matter how extensively it has fused with other world musics, is traced to Punjab. South Asian points of origin also connect the several diasporas that run parallel to the modern South Asian diaspora, not least among them the historical and musical journey of Roma people, which, as in the film *Latcho Drom* (1993), itself framed as a historical diaspora charted by music, began in Rajasthan.

Myth and religious narrative. The sacred and secular stories of South Asian music propel it along the path of diaspora. The stories of the *Rāmāyaṇa* and the *Mahābhārata* epic cycles open narrative spaces for Hindu mythology, and music, explicitly in song texts and formal structures, absorbs the stories. In the diaspora myth and religious narrative find their way to new settings, for example Hindu temples in North American suburbs, where new generations learn *bhajan*s, or in Sufi shrines of North England and Scotland, where new and old saints are praised by travelling troupes performing *qawwali*.

Classical music societies and classical dance companies. The institutional structures of colonial India frequently provided

Box 7 Select glossary of world musics shaped by diaspora

bhangra: historicized folk dance from Punjab (north-west India). In the South Asian diaspora, bhangra mixes styles that consciously invite fusion, for example in exchanges with reggae and Jamaican dance hall.

Bollywood: the music that accompanies Indian films of the same name. Originally applied to the Hindi-language films produced in 'Bombay', Indian film music is now an essential part of the transnational South Asian diaspora.

chutney: hybrid Caribbean popular music, especially in Trinidad, which combines styles from the South Asian and African diasporas. Chutney encompasses different sounds while mapping South Asian instruments on Afro-Caribbean festivals.

dangdut: Indonesian popular song, drawing its ethical content from Islam, the dominant religion of Indonesia, but its musical style from Bollywood songs.

ghazal: a poetic genre, usually employing couplets, that has spread across the Islamic world, from the Muslim Balkans and Turkey in the west to South Asia and South-East Asia in the east.

hip hop: originally a style of highly declaimed African American popular music, hip hop has spread globally as one of the most widespread of all popular musics in the 21st century.

klezmer: Jewish popular music, historically associated with the rituals and weddings in the Yiddish-speaking communities of Eastern Europe. Klezmer has entered a diaspora of its own that historicizes the world of European Jewry destroyed by the Holocaust.

mestizaje: general term describing the presence of Hispanic elements in Latinx popular musics. *Mestizaje* undergirds the complex patterns of hybridity that have propelled Latinx musics into the popular music mainstream of the Americas.

reggae: Jamaican dance music, shaped from the mediation of local dance styles, such as ska, through the mixing boards of dance hall disc jockeys.

taarab: the most widespread popular music along the multiple diasporic paths shared by the nations of the Indian Ocean littoral. *Taarab* repertories originally used Arabic-language lyrics, but since the mid-20th century circulate most extensively in Swahili and Hindi.

models for the organization of Indian classical music and dance. Supported by voluntary membership but not infrequently through government arts funding, these societies have become products of the diaspora, where they facilitate the consolidation of practices from across the regional and religious boundaries in South Asia.

Indian cinema. The Indian cinema is the most globalized site for the production and consumption of South Asian music. Often described with a variety of statistics as the largest film industry in the world—Ashish Rajadhyaksha cites UNESCO's estimate of 1,255 feature films per year, roughly one in five films shot worldwide—'Bollywood' relies extensively on film music. The incorporation of music into Indian film is nothing if not eclectic, and it has become one of the primary forms of musical entertainment in the diaspora, sold and rented as DVDs in grocery stores and newsstands, or available on the internet.

Popular music, fusion, and border crossing. Considered as a whole, the places of music in the South Asian diaspora form a landscape that encourages rather than stems change. Music defines place not by isolating it, but rather by opening stylistic borders. It is diasporic border crossing, for example, that produces 'chutney' in the Caribbean and bhangra in the United Kingdom, or the fusion soundscapes of Academy Award-winning film composer, A. R. Rahman (b. 1966). The place of music enriches the conditions for the processes of change that narrate the history of diaspora itself.

A. Z. Idelsohn and his musical monument of Jewish diaspora

Gathering the music of diaspora in a single anthology and publishing it as a representative monument of diaspora would seem like an improbable, surely futile, undertaking. This was, nonetheless, precisely the task that Abraham Zvi Idelsohn (1882–1938) set for himself in 1911, when he arrived in Jerusalem with a wax-disc recording machine from the Academy of Sciences of the Austro-Hungarian Empire. Over the course of the years leading to the First World War, Idelsohn would work and teach in Jerusalem to support the systematic recording of music sung and played in Jewish communities from throughout the diaspora—from Morocco in the west to Bukhara and Daghestan in the east—who were arriving in the *yishuv* (or 'settlement') in the eastern Mediterranean, at the time part of the Ottoman Empire.

The diaspora project occupied Idelsohn for the remainder of his life, shaping research and publication, and his teaching in Europe, the United States, and South Africa. The destabilizing of empire during the First World War, the rise of fascism and anti-Semitism, and several immigrations of his own did not deter Idelsohn from publishing his musical monument, the ten-volume *Thesaurus of Hebrew-Oriental Melodies*. Volume by volume, the *Thesaurus* moves systematically across the diaspora. The first five volumes encompassed the traditions of Jews from Yemen (vol. 1), Central Asia (vol. 3), and North Africa (vol. 5), among others.

With the second five volumes, Idelsohn returned to traditions that were closer to his own heritage as a Latvian-born cantor who had built a career in Germany, where he also studied musicology: here were volumes devoted to the 18th-century German synagogue (vol. 6), the folk songs of Eastern European Jews (vol. 9), and the songs of Hasidic Jews (vol. 10). Idelsohn transcribed and published his recordings, and he extracted melodies from manuscripts handed down by Jewish cantors or captured in transcriptions of folk music. He established historical connections and plotted them on systematic analytical tables. He applied theoretical models from historical musicology and comparative musicology, and he used the latest scientific methods to explore the extent to which the diaspora was unified by music. As archival sources for 20th-century Israeli composers and transformed into digitized CD anthologies, Idelsohn's *Thesaurus* continually affords new ways of sounding the diasporic past in the present.

Taarab—in search of the Indian Ocean diaspora

In June 2016, when I set out on foot in search of *taarab* music through the Stone Town district of the city of Zanzibar, I expected to discover it in what most observers had long described as its traditional habitation: an intimate music club set off from a narrow alley, modest in size and physical accommodations, with an audience largely of men listening to women soloists performing with a Middle Eastern-style small instrumental ensemble (see Chapter 3). I was disappointed not in the least, indeed, even delighted to witness confirmation of Janet Topp Fargion's documentation of the modern transition of *taarab* to a women's musical practice, also in the audiences of largely Muslim Zanzibar. There was, however, much about the *taarab* clubs in the Stone Town of 2016 that I had not expected.

If Stone Town provides an epicentre of locality and authenticity in the lore about *taarab*, the performances it supports are anything but local. Instead, *taarab*, performed live and in its presumed home, reveals the many strands of its long history as a popular music shaped at the intersections of many different diasporas. The material presence of instruments largely from the Middle East continues to narrate the religious and aesthetic impact of Islam. The social setting, too, remains one of intimate spaces formed during the centuries of Arabic, European, South Asian, and South-East Asian encounter.

There were also thoroughly modern aspects of mobility and hybridity. The lyrics of the songs, once in Arabic, had shifted to Swahili. Though women had not performed in early *taarab* ensembles in the late 19th and early 20th century, they had become the central figures in a popular music fully integrated into public spaces. Above all, there were the many elements of *taarab* that had come into being because of the technologies of exchange and globalization.

All of these elements come to the fore in the lives of the great musicians who made *taarab* global, none more so than Siti binti Saad (1880–1950). Growing up in rural Zanzibar, Siti binti Saad gradually won favour as a singer in urban ensembles, albeit in traditional roles. In 1928, soon after the introduction of electronic microphones, she travelled to India to dedicate herself to intensive recording of *taarab* in the colonial studios of Columbia Records and His Master's Voice. We now trace the transformation of *taarab* through the more than 150 recordings she made in Bombay, from the canonization of Swahili to the studio mixing of Middle Eastern and North Indian instruments. Musically, still today, *taarab* sounds the elements of many homes and multiple diasporas, all of which reside comfortably together in the popular music of the Indian Ocean.

Chapter 7
Empire, decoloniality, and the globalization of world music

Street music at the edge of empire

Early each weekday and Saturday morning, merchants gather in the marketplace of Cluj Napoca, Romania, to sell their wares. Surrounded by the sterile and crumbling cement edifices that make it difficult to forget the former imperial economies competing for the lands of Transylvania, the merchants of the Cluj marketplace sell everything, old and new, locally produced and globally manufactured. There is a patina of pastness and folkloric authenticity pervading the marketplace. In many stalls sumptuous leather and fur goods are for sale, and cloth goods piled high catch the eye because of the colourful needlework that leads one to believe they are produced by craftspeople from the Carpathian Mountains dominating central Transylvania, where Cluj is the capital city. Four languages are woven together in the discussions about the sale of goods: Romanian, Hungarian, 'Ruthenian' (the Slavic language of the central Carpathians), and Romany (the Indo-European language of the Roma). There is no *lingua franca* in this marketplace, not even German and English, both of which are also heard.

Music is everywhere in the Cluj marketplace, very much a participant in the culture of commerce. Loudspeakers blare, and radios contribute to the electronic counterpoint. Some merchants have CDs for sale, and more than a few offer handcrafted instruments, usually flutes made from wood or clay, but also more elaborate stringed instruments. Musicians ply the aisles, wending their ways through labyrinthine booths. The musicians know only too well just where they can set up their portable stages to attract the most generous audiences. They know which repertories will best sell to Cluj's many students, and they are sensitive to not making a false step by drawing attention to the long-standing frictions between Romanian- and Hungarian-speaking residents. The street musicians are even more aware of the growing numbers of tourists who are visiting Transylvania since Romania joined the European Union in 2007. Eastern Europe entered a period of dizzying transition in the 1990s and thereafter during the 21st century, and Romania's street musicians were quick to make the most of it (Figure 10).

10. Street musician in a marketplace in Bucharest, Romania (1998).

The street music of Cluj Napoca is world music in the most modern sense. It is global music performed locally. Its juxtapositions and unpredictable stylistic hybridity are postmodern. If one looks and listens long enough, one will encounter musical evidence gathered from the edges of empires throughout the world. The street musicians are professionals, and their stock in trade is a capacity to adapt themselves to the changing currents of a multicultural society. The street music of Cluj is also traditional. In their home villages on weekends musicians also play for dances, weddings, or other rituals constituting traditional folk culture. Whereas many musicians rely on recent technologies, say, for managing their own websites, they also play instruments made by local instrument builders. Where else would they find handiwork to rival that of the local bagpipe maker?

The crucial point is not that these street musicians are *both* world musicians *and* traditional folk musicians, but rather that they have collapsed the difference between the two. The complex roles of Cluj's street musicians should not surprise us. Cluj Napoca's modernity and decoloniality are the products of its past, that is, of its cultural accommodation to the Austro-Hungarian Empire, to the contested cultures of Hungarians and Romanians, and to a plethora of minority groups. So culturally complex was the past that the city has three names even today: Cluj Napoca (Romanian), Kolozsvár (Hungarian), and Klausenburg (German). In the opening decades of the 21st century the encounter with world music has become an everyday experience. There is, however, a paradox that lurks in the forms of encounter that generate globalization. If indeed we share world music globally through our encounter with it, we nonetheless experience it in very different worlds, which in turn are shaped in distinctively different ways because of economic, ethnic and racial, political and historical disparities. There are today more different technologies that enable us to encounter more world music than ever before, but the question arises as to whether these facilitate or complicate encounter. To whom, we increasingly find ourselves asking, do the everyday worlds of world music really belong?

The global city and world music history

The global city is the entrepôt for the encounters with world music in a postmodern world. Throughout history the city has occupied a distinctive position on the musical landscape because of the diversity it could attract. The musical life of the premodern city possessed the traits of a pre-world music. In a city dominated by trade, say, along Saharan trade routes in Africa or along the Silk Road across Asia, the merchants passing through them were frequently accompanied by musicians and musical goods. As the premodern city gave way to the modern city, it developed from a musical marketplace to a site for more extensive production and consumption of music. As print culture affected the production of music, particularly during the Age of Discovery and the expansion of European empires from the 16th to the late 18th century, new forms of specialization exerted a profound effect on the diversity nourishing a city's musical life. It was in the 19th and 20th centuries, however, that urban culture underwent an explosion of worldwide proportions. Cities multiplied in number and grew in size. As the disintegration of colonial empires accelerated in the 20th century, international metropolises—what we now call 'global cities'—arose as the sites of global encounter, dominating the map of world music.

There is no single type of encounter in the global city, thus the types of world music we encounter are virtually unlimited. The modern city gave the individual a greater degree of freedom to move about in the public spaces of the metropolis. The German philosopher Walter Benjamin (1892–1940) theorized the individual's encounters with the culture of the city by employing the metaphor of the shopping arcade in the Paris of the 19th century. The individual walking through the shopping streets of the city comes to know its culture by gazing at the display windows and hearing the fragments of conversation exchanged between passers-by. Music, too, is a part of the encounters made possible by the shopping arcade, for its arteries pass in front of cafés with music, theatres, and street musicians. At first glance, such individual encounters might seem random, but Benjamin suggests that they are placed in patterns by the city itself, transformed to produce 'sounding cities'.

The global city belies the claims for global 'grey-out', because musical diversity in the 21st century is greater than ever before. It is clear that the old models of immigrant culture, with the traces of the 'old country' disappearing after three generations, were overly simplified. Musicians in the global city do not just perform in public or private settings, but rather they form complex affiliations that cut across socioeconomic, religious, and ethnic boundaries. The music cultures of cities today demonstrate patterns of ethnic, racial, and religious diversity that differ from one another, but grow from the distinctive ways that each city accommodates emigration from the outside, migration within the city, and the constant remixing of old and new neighbourhoods.

My reference at the beginning of this section to the city as an 'entrepôt' for world music was not simply a rhetorical gesture. In its original sense an entrepôt was a warehouse that served as a point for gathering goods that would be made available for sale. The encounters with world music in the city, too, are connected in complex ways to the marketing of world music. In the premodern city music acquired its diversity quite literally in the marketplace. The shops that lined Benjamin's arcades were places of business. Street musicians determine where and when they perform in large part according to financial benefits. The economies of world music consumption also inform the remaining sections of this chapter, for musical tourism and the festivalization of world music are, at base, economically motivated. And if they were not, they would not have spread across the global musical landscape of the 21st century.

Wedding musicians in Kolkata

Wedding musicians are among the most globally ubiquitous musical specialists in the world. Their craft is essential for enacting ritual and for weaving sacred, secular, and social practices together. They possess a form of musical knowledge that is individual and yet broadly common across culture and religion. Their mobility affords many possibilities for moving between and among different classes, socioeconomic groups, and even religions. Entire genres of music and classes of musical specialists can be associated with performance at weddings—klezmer musicians in the Ashkenazic Jewish tradition or transgender *hijra* musicians in South Asia, for instance. Their command of different repertories and ability to sell them for financial gain might well lead us to designate them as global musicians par excellence.

The extent of the globalization mobilizing wedding musicians in the 21st century is fully evident in the professional trade that annually accompanies India's wedding season. Weddings take place at times that are seasonally and religiously auspicious in many parts of the world. In Hindu tradition the most auspicious season begins with the onset of Sarasvatī Pūjā, the festival associated with the goddess of music, knowledge, art, and science, which begins in the dark months of midwinter, and stretches to the festival of Holi, marking the onset of spring at the time of its first full moon. Music, especially in the representation of Sarasvatī holding a *vīṇā* in performing position, remains central to the historical meaning of the wedding season (see Figure 2).

It is into this seemingly traditional narrative of the past that wedding musicians have introduced new symbols and meanings. Though it is impossible to know exactly when earlier wedding musicians adopted ritual practices as their own and adapted them for the professional marketplace, several forms of physical evidence strongly suggest that the earliest stage took place during the British colonial period. Already in the 19th century, the

11. Twenty-first-century wedding musicians in Kolkata.

instruments that appear in photographs of wedding bands are those of British military bands. The uniforms used by wedding bands, too, bear witness to a heritage of interaction with colonial military ensembles (see Figure 11). The historical record further contains photographs documenting the extent to which colonized South Asians filled the ranks of musical ensembles with administrative functions in the Raj. Public spectacle—parades, government ceremonies, mustering soldiers to fight in proxy wars for the empire—became sites for the performance of musics gathered from the empire's new global cities, such as Bombay and Calcutta.

The past may influence aspects of today's wedding musicians in the global cities of 21st-century Mumbai and Kolkata, but as they pass through accelerating decolonizing processes so too do other forms of hybridity. The wedding musicians who perform during Sarasvatī Pūjā in Kolkata, for example, migrate annually to the city from elsewhere, mostly from neighbouring Bihar state. They are overwhelmingly Muslim, and they speak Hindi,

Bhojpuri, Maithili, as well as other languages from Bihar, but only rarely Bangla, the language of Kolkata. The wedding musicians are outsiders and therefore must find a temporary neighbourhood to market their trade. Since at least the beginning of modern Indian statehood in 1947, one of the most important urban arteries of north Kolkata, Mahatma Gandhi Road, has served this function.

The different bands stake out quarters along MG Road, in which instruments and uniforms are stored. Open to the street itself, the small quarters—kiosks of no more than a few square metres—invite potential wedding parties to enter and bring with them a musical wedding theme for their own ceremony, maybe a repertory of sacred music, but far more likely a CD with Bollywood songs or Western popular music in the soundtrack from a well-known movie. Once the theme is chosen, band members go about intensively learning their parts from oral tradition for the upcoming ceremony. Through their performance on the streets of Kolkata the wedding musicians enact a new moment of globalization, a hybrid narrative of India's past and present in a complex world.

Recording and the technologies of globalization

Imagine for a moment what an ethnomusicologist's gallery of fieldwork would contain. On one wall there would be photographs of the people the ethnomusicologist had studied. On another there might be artefacts brought back from the field, surely musical instruments and more than likely other kinds of ritual artefacts. Then there would probably be an area in front of the third wall with display cases in which the 'music itself' was gathered, the transcriptions, tapes, and videos documenting their fieldwork. Finally, there would be an area devoted to the technologies that made the fieldwork possible, with display cases full of recording machines and cameras, and with a wall devoted to photographs of the ethnomusicologist in the act of recording.

An imaginary museum of ethnomusicological research? Hardly. A retrospective exhibit on fieldwork in an age of decoloniality? Indeed that, but more as well. Ethnomusicologists have always displayed a penchant for showing the tools of their trade and documenting the technologies that allowed them to turn the field into a laboratory. The photographs of ethnomusicologists recording singers and musicians, and collecting interviews and performances could fill volumes devoted to the field's history. Dominating the photographs of the ethnomusicologist at work is not so much its human aspect as the machine itself, given pride of place in order to document something crucial about encountering world music. The recording machine is there to make a statement about authenticity, power, and the potential of the individual scholar to enter the field as an ethnomusicologist.

If we wanted to write a history of ethnomusicology as a response to specific technological advances, it would not be difficult. As a discipline, modern ethnomusicology has come to depend on what Walter Benjamin called the 'age of mechanical reproduction'. Technology mediates the encounter with world music, and with each technological advance ethnomusicologists gain a sense that they can gather more details about world music. Arguably, ethnomusicology has gained in prestige because advancing technologies have allowed the field to claim a more rigorous scientific basis. There are subdisciplines within ethnomusicology that rely almost entirely on technologies to mediate music as data for objective interpretation. Systematic musicologists trace their intellectual genealogy to 19th- and 20th-century scholars such as Alexander Ellis, who devised a system for dividing musical scales into equal frequency measurements, or 'cents', and to Carl Stumpf, the German psychologist who established the first laboratory devoted to analysing recordings in the Berlin Phonogram Archive.

By no means is the systematic impulse in ethnomusicology solely dedicated to the scientific description of sound. Establishing the parameters of authenticity is equally a motivation. Can the analysis of the sound itself reveal more about what we hear and interpret as music? Can the physics of music, the representation of music as wave-form and timbral display, transform our understanding of the metaphysics of music? Recording technology allows us to think in different ways about what authenticity might be. The question arises as to whether discussions about the ethics of recording and technology can keep up with the blinding pace of technological advance. The digital technologies flooding the global music market during the 1990s made it possible for almost anyone to encounter world music on CDs and on the internet, and the sheer welter of recordings overwhelmed the legal encumbrances that might have given the listener pause for considering the ethical dimensions of world music. As ethical dilemmas they differ only in kind from the concerns about power, appropriation, and cultural conflict that have always accompanied encounters with world music. If they arise from the technological sectors of the ethnomusicological endeavour, they are no less insistent that ethnomusicologists accept the moral responsibility of scholarship today.

The *Rough Guides*—mapping world music in the 21st century

As if there were lingering doubts that world music had come of age with the 21st century, the *Rough Guides to World Music* rebut them from the start. In no uncertain terms the *Rough Guides* celebrate their own comprehensiveness: world music is boundless and boundaryless, and its soundscapes contain 'the oldest and newest music in the world'. If their claims ring a bit heraldic, the *Rough Guides* volumes nonetheless provide extensive documentation of the postmodern encounter with world music. The *Rough Guides* are as much advertisement—for musicians who tour the world, their recording companies, and the travel industry that sponsors the world-hopping musical tourism—as real guides to the diversity of musical phenomena. The *Rough Guides* themselves appear in two formats, voluminous books that take the reader on musical tours to different parts of the world (e.g. vol. 2, *Latin and North America, Caribbean, India, Asia and Pacific*) and CD anthologies that are both regionally general and genre specific (e.g. *Salsa* and *Salsa Dance*). Ultimately, the *Rough Guides* concern themselves far more with facilitating virtual encounter with the world of music than with world music itself.

My use of the term 'virtual encounter' might seem suggestive of technologies out of control and of music reduced to mediation. Anyone who turns to the *Rough Guides* or downloads individual albums quickly finds reasons to draw attention to their lacunae. Even within academic ethnomusicology, most of us love to hate the ways the *Rough Guides* reduce discourse about world music to so many quick-and-dirty blurbs, but few of us would deny that those blurbs often come in handy. It is possible to open the *Rough Guides* just about anywhere to follow their maps of ethnomusicological encounter today. As nationalism spreads in many parts of the world, recordings have emerged as an important context for supporting or resisting it. Globally, the digital availability of recordings in the cloud (e.g. from Spotify) is perhaps the most vital discourse for sonically representing diaspora.

The *Rough Guides* also serve as a guide, perhaps unintentionally, to recent directions in ethnomusicology. Most obviously, they are guides primarily to popular music, and there can be little question that no area of ethnomusicology has grown as rapidly and become as influential in the 21st century as popular music studies. Developing in large part from the *Rough Guides*' privileging of popular music is a discourse that embraces hybridity, fusion, and border crossing, in other words the inescapable conditions of globalization. The *Rough Guides*, both books and recorded collections, could be confused for a purist's bible or soundtracks of authenticity by no one, but here too there is a message, perhaps a bitter one to the purist clinging to an older gospel. Finally, there can be no question that the maps of global encounter are themselves vastly different. World music intensifies in immigrant and exile communities; it lends itself to ideological manipulation across the spectrum of political power; it affixes itself to revivalism no less than to experimentalism; it is the stuff of festival culture and tourism.

World music festivals—at home in the world

15 February 2019, a moment in the ethnographic present when history returns. As I complete the final sections for this book, the 59th Annual University of Chicago Folk Festival is about to begin. As they do every year, the organizers of the festival have once again invited participants who will present concerts, lead workshops, or transform the university campus into a sonic map of the world and those who most fully represent the diversity of world music. Diversity embraces genre—blues, bluegrass, klezmer, jazz—and it stretches across place—from Chicago to Ireland to Cajun Louisiana. The oldest university folk festival in the world, its 59th return is the latest chapter in a historical response to global events that began during the Cold War, and it mounts a response to the rise of illiberal nationalism in the present. Over the many years of the festival, the organizers have dedicated themselves to representing diversity as capaciously as possible—ethnic, racial, religious, gender. They cross the boundaries between styles and nations; they celebrate the transformational impact of changing media; and they seek integration in forms idealized and practical, turning the day-by-day tasks of running the festival over to students, who make world music their own, each year on this weekend, in their home.

The ways in which world music inhabits our homes also bear witness to its histories of past and present, especially in the moments of encounter, celebration, and exchange constituting the parallel histories of festival. It is at these moments that the home and the world become one. Chicago has a particularly long history of festivals in which world music was gathered and deployed across the city. We might understand this domestication of world music in different ways, but suffice it to say that the city's cultural planners have sought to sustain diversity and afford it spaces on the city soundscape for almost two centuries.

We have already visited the Chicago World's Columbian Exposition in earlier chapters of this book (e.g. Chapter 6), but we revisit it here because of its influence on the ways festivals have brought music to the home. It was at the Columbian Exposition that the first set of audio recordings to which we can refer as world music was made, wax cylinders used by the team led by Benjamin Ives Gilman and Franz Boas. Musicians came from throughout the world, many of them famous in their countries (e.g. Georg Dänzer (1848–93), a member of Vienna's most celebrated popular music ensemble in the 19th century, the Schrammel-Quartett, who died on the return trip from Chicago), others unknown and neglected. During the summer and early autumn of 1893, Chicago became a global home to world music. Exhibit halls, theatres, concert halls, and cafés spread across the south side of the city, leaving their global material imprint on the city and on festivals ever since (see Figure 12). The pavilions of empire created a north–south axis along the Lake Michigan shoreline, while venues of world music and entertainment stretched along the east–west corridor of the Midway Plaisance, already in 1893 intersecting the University of Chicago campus. To travel the streets of the Columbian Exposition and to pass along its waterways was to experience the world aurally. Home and the world were made one.

Festivals and fairs would return year after year to Chicago, drawing upon its musical and cultural diversity. These global moments would provide opportunities for Chicago musicians to give music to the world. The first collections of Irish folk music, eventually published in a ten-volume canon containing thousands of melodies, began with Francis O'Neill (1848–1938), the Irish-born police superintendent whose recordings appeared initially in the years after the Columbian Exposition. There would

12. **1893 Map of the World's Columbian Exposition in Chicago.**

be another world's fair in Chicago, the Century of Progress, in 1933, at which the city's role as a home for blues and jazz after the 'Great Migration' of African Americans from the American South, but especially their global dissemination on the labels of Chicago recording companies, would be celebrated.

Chicago's history of bringing world music close to home gives us pause to reflect on the festival of world music as just another instance of the victimization of Indigenous and local musicians to buttress the reach of transnational music distribution. We would see world music close to home in such light only if we treated it monolithically, as a single event, each return no more nor less than a metaphor for the hegemony of the West. A festival is not, however, a single, concentrated moment for the performance of world music. It results, rather, from the confluence of many different histories.

If I close this chapter with an ethnographic moment, close to home, it is to remind readers that they need not look far or wait very long before having the opportunity to witness world music in a festival close to home. The types of encounter and exchange brought about by a world music festival are not new. Some forms of encounter have disappeared, but others have increased in number and variety. There is little—I should argue, no—evidence that the abundant ways of encountering world music today show any signs of abating. If we examine the encounters that fill a world music festival today more ethnographically, as ethnomusicologists but also as global citizens in the 21st century, we recognize that the music that sounds our homes has the potential to remap the world. Each of us—ethnomusicologist, musician, avid amateur, passive listener—continues to encounter the music of the world in a growing variety of ways, drawing us ineluctably into a world, the identity and culture of which is no longer separable from our own lives, at home in the world.

Chapter 8
World music matters

World music materiality

By almost anyone's geographical standards the location of the Indian village of Dadpur is remote. Lying in the tropical forests on the flood plains of the Ganges River delta in the state of West Bengal, Dadpur is reachable only after a journey of three or four hours from Kolkata, the cultural megacity and political capital of West Bengal. After a train journey of several hours, one must travel by car to the point at which an auto-rickshaw resumes the journey to the edge of the forests, beyond which it is only possible to follow a footpath through the fields that periodically flood during the monsoon months. The soil and the flora of the lands surrounding the village form an ecosystem for the Ganges delta, and they yield the raw materials upon which Dadpur's *c.*80 residents depend for their livelihood.

In one way or other, everyone in Dadpur is engaged in making musical instruments. There are those who gather the materials that become parts of the instruments created in the village workshops, the gourds used for resonating chambers, the woods for the bodies, and the lacquers and decoration that enhance an instrument's visual beauty (see Figure 13). String instruments of many kinds line the walls of the workshops—large sitars for the soloists and *tanpuras* for the accompanists in Hindustani classical

13. Instrument maker, Dadpur, West Bengal, India (2012).

music, as well as violins and guitars, made to order for various genres of Western music. Just as Dadpur lies at the end of a journey to a remote village, the instruments made by its local craftspeople begin their journey there. The first leg of the journey brings them to Kolkata, a regional, national, and global centre for instrument-making. Some of Dadpur's instruments end up in the hands of Bengali musicians. Others find their way to music shops across India. Still others are purchased by wholesalers to be sold internationally.

The world music network that the instrument makers of this remote village set in motion has its origins in the materiality of a natural world, yet depends on the ways that material becomes music for those unfamiliar with the soils, fields, and forests from which their instruments were forged. In this final chapter, we turn to the materiality of world music with attention to the ways it is critical to the network encompassing the natural world in all its dimensions and the world made and occupied by human inhabitants, the Anthropocene (from the Greek, ἄνθρωπος—human + καινός—new). In the 21st century, these worlds are at great risk, through climate change, global warming, and the destruction of the material substance of nature itself.

Dadpur lies in one of the most endangered areas of the global Anthropocene. If the seas of the Bay of Bengal rise only minimally, they will soon consume the Ganges delta. Neither the village nor the ecosystem that provides materials necessary to the global network of musical instruments it produces will survive. The successive material nodes that form the global network for disseminating the instruments are themselves no less endangered. The arteries of commerce connecting Dadpur to Kolkata will be swallowed by rising water, and Kolkata, so precariously perched on the banks of the Hooghly River since founded as a commercial entrepôt in the late 17th century, will prove no match against climate catastrophe.

These are matters of material concern—of musical material and why music therefore matters as we face the threat to the Anthropocene in the 21st century. At first glance, the musical materiality that matters so much for Dadpur may seem like an unfortunate condition of its remoteness. Its connectedness—the counterpoint of journeys formed by instruments and their creators—tells another story, one increasingly central to what world music means in the 21st century. The title of the final chapter, therefore, has multiple meanings, which swell in a counterpoint of their own. 'Matter', on one hand, refers to the substance of 'material' and the materiality of music. On the other, matter also bears the force of 'importance', as in 'to make something matter'. It is not by chance that both meanings capture the spirit of social and political movements in our own day, for example, 'Black Lives Matter' and its activist response to racism in the United States. The multiple meanings further sustain concepts that have shaped the narrative of this book from its earliest chapters, for example, world music's uniting of object—materiality—and subject—mattering. It is because world music matters that we listen with increasing urgency to the narratives sounded in the common world we together inhabit.

Movable counterpoint—the global journey of encounter

Time, like place, also has its remote moments, far removed from the present, and yet also woven into a network that matters for the real-time sounded by world music. Music's residence at remote moments in the past has assumed many forms throughout the early chapters of this book. The transition of myth to history often follows the path of world music's growing materiality, for example, when oral tradition is inscribed through written texts and musical notation, or when the music from one part of the world moves to other parts on recorded media. For music archaeologists, time begins and becomes history with the material evidence—instruments, depictions of ritual, decipherings of sound in nature—at the deepest strata of the physical past.

World music, therefore, matters when it draws the remote past into the present, affording it new life in real-time. In search of the historical path between past and present I turn now to the life of a single song, a ballad that has circulated in multiple languages through Europe from the Middle Ages to the present. As he gathered the songs that would cohere as the first anthology of modern world music in 1778, Herder, too, turned to the ballad and published it in multiple variants (songs 7–11) in the collections entitled *Volkslieder*. The Spanish *romance*, 'Zaid and Zaida', captured Herder's attention for several reasons. As a ballad, it contained stories both fictional and historical, specific and flexible in their narrative details. A story of encounter between Islam and Christianity, the ballad was one among many tales of nationhood

Box 8 'Zaid and Zaida'

Through the streets on which his lady lived
Zaid paced back and forth,
Waiting for the hour to come,
Finally to come, so that he might speak with her.

And, in doubt, the Moor was already thinking
That it had been such a long delay,
He thought: If I could but once glance upon her,
All my flames would be quelled.

And then he saw her there!
She approached the window like the sun
Rising after the storm,
Like the moon rising in the night.

Quietly Zaid drew closer to her:
Allah be with you, lovely Moor!
Is it true, what my pages,
What your servants say?

'Zaid und Zaida' (Song 8 in J. G. Herder's *Volkslieder* [1778]; translated by the author in *Song Loves the Masses*, 75–7)

Herder had chosen for his song collections, among them his translation of the Spanish national epic, *El Cid*; 'Cid' and 'Zaid' are, in fact, variants of the same name, the Arabic 'Saʿid' (Box 8)

The history Herder might have attempted to realize by publishing variants of 'Zaid and Zaida' in a modern edition would move in directions even he did not predict. As a ballad with a captivity narrative, the story of the lovers, Zaid and Zaida, also captured the attention of other writers and musicians in Enlightenment Europe, among them Jean-Philippe Rameau and Wolfgang Amadeus Mozart, who set to work on a dramatic work for the musical stage, a *Singspiel*, calling it *Zaide*. It is quite likely that Mozart knew

Herder's translations, which appeared at the same moment he was preparing his own *Zaide*, with the same theme. Mozart gathered the arias and dramatic scenes he had completed by 1780, however leaving *Zaide* incomplete and turning instead to his better-known opera about encounter between Europe and the Mediterranean, *The Abduction from the Seraglio* (K. 384), which was premiered in 1782.

It is the unfinished history of *Zaide* that is of interest in this final chapter because of the context in which it returns in the real-time of the 21st-century refugee crisis faced by so many from the Mediterranean, Africa, and Middle East. Contemporary performances capture the long history of the folk ballad and opera, extending the Andalusian, Arabic, Spanish, Herderian, Mozartian history to the present. In performances across Germany, called *Zaide, eine Flucht* (Zaide, a refugee's journey), it is, in fact, *Flüchtlinge*, 'refugees' seeking safety in Europe from conflict in the Middle East, who weave their histories into a new performance for European audiences. Professional opera singers and refugees together interweave improvised recitatives about daily dangers and the difficulties of crossing national borders into the arias and ensemble songs composed by Mozart for *Zaide*. These refugee and non-refugee modern operatic performers realize a new counterpoint, reimagining world music anew in the real-time of their world in the 21st century.

World musicians matter

The global soundscapes of music have arisen from the movement and mobility of musicians throughout history, and it is no different today, when the movement of immigrants and refugees increasingly charts the history of the present. In the course of this book the mobility of music has taken many forms that realize the topography of world music. Folk songs move from one community to the next, and then beyond to lands and continents far removed from their origins. Diaspora results from the movement of peoples determined to hold onto the music that provides the temporary comfort of a new home. Music is in motion with pilgrims, street musicians, the armies of empire, and the faithful in search of utopia. Music's inherent mobility affords it the agency to effect diversity, dialogue, and the transnational networks of world music.

In the 21st century, even the most hopeful potential of music's mobility must confront growing challenges, many of them endangering the lives of world musicians. The routes and borders previously opened for the passage of migrants during moments of crisis have closed at an alarming rate. During a historical moment when the expansion of diaspora has accelerated, new national and international laws have been enacted to limit and prevent it. Previous zones of encounter and exchange, such as the Mediterranean (see Chapter 3), become zones of danger and death. The global metaphor for the new conditions of music's mobility is the wall, which, too, is material and physical, positioned across the world to silence immigrants, refugees, and world musicians.

Music's inherent mobility, however, is not so easily brought to a standstill. Just as the physical presence of new walls along the borders separating European nations from the lands of refugees, or those keeping Palestinians from Israel and Central Americans from the United States, seemingly enforce silence, so too are there new voices from world musicians, mobilizing the musics that resist silence. In the long history of borders there have been genres of music (e.g. 'captivity ballads') that narrate the ways in which captive peoples have gained their freedom, from the biblical Psalm 137 ('By the waters of Babylon') to modern operas such as Mozart's *Abduction from the Seraglio* and Beethoven's *Fidelio* (Op. 72). In North American folk music, the Spanish-language genre, *corrido*, circulates widely as border ballads from the physical zones of US American–Mexican encounter. Rather than being blocked by the physical encumbrances of border exclusion, global musical practices, such as the popular music of Tuareg musicians in Mali or Malagasy musicians in Madagascar, realize new materiality and mobility.

The mobility and materiality of world music also afforded response to the immigrant and refugee crisis that followed the conflicts that swept Syria, Somalia, Afghanistan, and other lands torn apart by political and military conflict in the early 21st century. The sonic topography that migrant musicians charted in Europe has borne witness to several distinctive sites and genres of refugee and immigrant music, three of which are particularly prominent. Initially, there are the sites of *dispersion* in the lands from which refugees were fleeing, in which new genres of music coalesced and mediated transnationally. The political and musical message of the different national resistance movements in North Africa and the Middle East following the Arab Spring (2011–13) found its way quickly to hip-hop artists. Through the extensive dispersion of radio, television, and, especially, the internet, Arab rappers mobilized international styles into regional and national styles. Local and regional styles also dispersed in the opposite direction, transported by refugees beyond the borders and walls erected by conflict. The most striking example of a regional music and dance style that spread from the Levant, or Eastern Mediterranean, to Europe is the Syrian *dabke*, which provided symbolic unity to the more than one million refugees from Syria and the Middle East finding temporary homes in Germany after 2015.

The sonic topography of the refugee crisis also accrued to the physical sites of *departure and passage*. The way stations outside the walls of impermeable borders and networks of refugee camps often became sites of music making and global community united against oppression. The most famous case of a refugee camp transformed into a musical microcosm was the 'Jungle', an extensive community of migrants seeking transit from continental Europe to the United Kingdom, located along the docks of Calais, France.

Though it flourished during 2015 and 2016, the Jungle was eventually forcibly dismantled, but its impact on the music culture of a Europe shaped by refugees spread across the continent's borders. Under the best of circumstances refugees underwent transformation into immigrants, with the fortunate able to settle in more welcoming nations, such as Germany and the Nordic countries. In cosmopolitan cities such as Paris and Berlin it has become possible to speak of a new *transnational diaspora*. Berliners can even lay claim to a cultural infrastructure that has supported immigrant ensembles (e.g. the Babylon Orchestra), has opened music schools for teaching world music (e.g. the Turkish Music Conservatory), and has sustained festivals dedicated to the musics of Islamicate cultures and lands, notably the 'Nächte des Ramadan' (Nights of Ramadan).

Sound matters

Sound moves between and among the materials that together represent the ontologies of time and instruments of the South Asian soundscape in the *Nāṭyaśāstra*, the treatise on music, theatre, and dance whose earliest versions date from roughly the 3rd century CE (Box 9). Sound emanates from multiple origins in nature, and then comes to reside in and re-sound through the artifice of objects transformed by human action. The affordances of aesthetic attributes accrue to sound through human perception and reason. Sound objects are collected, constructed, and calibrated, closing the borders between the natural and human worlds, conjoining their temporal worlds as music to engender the complex system of metre in South Asian music, *tāla*.

Encounters with world music have long expanded the ontologies of sound, deriving aesthetic meaning from the materiality of sounding objects. In this section we turn to the study of music as sound, identifying historical origins in descriptions of world music while also seeking connections to the more recent emphasis on sonic experience beyond music, especially in the field of sound studies. The questions that arise at the confluence of historical and contemporary sound studies are aesthetic and culturally constitutive, varying, sometimes considerably, across time and space. And yet, there are ways in which they bear witness to common aesthetic attributes in the materiality of sound and music. The authors—Bharata-Muni was most likely a name given to a fictional collective of contributors—who contributed to the *Nāṭyaśāstra*, for example, proposed a system for classifying musical instruments according to the four material substances from which they were constructed and that shape the means whereby they set sound in motion—using stretched membrane surfaces (as in Box 9), columns of air, tightened strings (as in Dadpur), and solid substances that sound themselves.

Sound matters across the aesthetic ontologies of world music because it is perceived in such varied ways. Broadly speaking, there are three sites from which sound originates on its conceptual path toward meaning and music. The first of these is the *body*, in which sound emanates from within and without. We experience sound internally, listening with an 'inner ear', transforming symbols external to the body into hearing. We also create sound with our bodies, which in turn is heard by others. The *environment* is the second general source for sound. Human beings live in a world of sounds, natural and artificial. Living in a sounded world requires countless acts of ordering sound itself. In the passage from the *Nāṭyaśāstra* (Box 9), the hermit follows a chain of events giving order to environmental sound, eventually translating it to the temporal ordering of *tāla* played by drums. The final general source for sound, like the drums in the *Nāṭyaśāstra*, is *mediating materiality*. Material is generally not in and of itself a sound object, but it becomes so through acts of mediation when sound subjects act upon material. Mediation multiplies the ontologies immanent in materiality and expands the aesthetic realm through which sound moves.

Box 9 ***Nāṭyaśāstra*****—The origin of drums**

Now following Svāti I shall speak briefly about the origin and development of musical instruments called Puskaras (drums).

During an intermission of studies in the rainy season, Svāti once went to a lake for fetching water...

Then in this lake, torrents of water falling with the force of wind made clear sounds on the leaves of lotus...

After observing the high, medium and low sounds produced on the lotus-leaves as deep, sweet and pleasing, he went back to his hermitage... [where he] covered these and Mrdanga, Dardura and Panava with hide, and bound them with strings.

(Bharata-Muni, *The Nāṭyaśāstra*, vol. 2: 161–2)

The constituent fields of 21st-century sound studies reflect these three broad approaches to understanding the origins of sound. Among the constituent fields those with the longest tradition have been listening studies and voice studies. Central to their aesthetic concerns is the complementarity of sounding and listening. We have seen such concerns at work in approaches to sound and music in Islam, the dual meaning of *samā'* as 'hearing' and 'listening', each specifying different forms of agency. Most recently, such approaches may begin with the body, but they expand the very concept of what the body does, through movement and cognition, and because of the affordances of disability.

Recognition that humans live in a sonic environment has considerably transformed music's epistemologies in 21st-century theory. Ethnomusicologists in particular have begun to investigate the ways sound not only derives meaning from place, but also gives meaning to place, by employing approaches to sound studies gathered under concepts such as 'acoustemology' (Steven Feld) and 'aurality' (Ana María Ochoa Gautier). Sonic environments are also the product of human artifice, for example, in the study of cities as urban environments, in which sound shapes ritual, everyday time, and history.

Musical material and media themselves are increasingly important to sound studies. When sound studies scholars look at ways in which materials such as electronic tape, digital storage units, or electronically enhanced musical instruments mediate sound, they direct our interest toward the processes that transform sounding objects so that they have meaning for musical subjectivities. These processes open new ontologies of sound, thereby also leading to the proliferation of agency in order that music matters both for those who produce it and those who receive it.

Intangible Cultural Heritage—making world music matter

Ethnomusicologists rarely travel alone when in search of world music. We are joined by those increasingly recognized for sharing their knowledge, experience, and music, coequals at moments of encounter. Experiencing world music involves exchange in all directions, listening and hearing, creating sound and letting it transform the spaces around one. The coequal presence of musicians, audiences, ethnomusicologists, and the natural worlds they cohabit serves as a critical theme in this final chapter. In search of that coequal presence I travel myself first to several ethnographic moments I shared while in India, and I then return to reflect on several recent global endeavours dedicated to sustaining the musicians who accompany ethnomusicologists and make music matter.

We have already briefly encountered the Bāuls of Indian West Bengal and Bangladesh when recognizing their importance as inspiration for Rabindranath Tagore (see Chapter 4). When I travel through West Bengal today, the Bāuls are no less present than they were for Tagore and the Bengali Renaissance. Like Tagore there were others who listened to the songs of the Bāuls and Bôyātis, among the most notable the mystical poet, Lālôn (*c.*1774–1890), and the Bangladeshi poet, Kazi Nazrul Islam (1899–1976). My journeys with Bāul musicians take place while travelling to Santiniketan in West Bengal, the cultural centre built by Rabindranath Tagore. As Bāuls move about the countryside and the villages around Santiniketan, they realize the material landscape of Bengal as the sonic world of their songs. Bāuls and Bôyātis seek those willing to join them and share all that Bāul music has come to mean (see Figure 14).

The coequal presence of Bāul musicians in the past and present in Bengal has been recognized far beyond India and Bangladesh, and in ways even more transnational than the songs and poetry of Lālôn, Tagore, and Nazrul Islam. In 2008, the Bāuls and their mystical tradition of song were officially included on the UNESCO Representative List of Intangible Cultural Heritage of Humanity, placed on that list as representatives of Bangladesh. 'Intangible Cultural Heritage' (ICH) was established by a UNESCO

14. Bôyāti (l.) and Bāul (r.) musicians in performance, Santiniketan, India.

convention in 2003, when it cast its nets widely, identifying the culture in need of protection as language, the performing arts, social and religious practices, and Indigenous knowledge generally. Critical to the agenda of the ICH offices located in Paris was a process of transforming the intangible into the material, a form of agency that could capture global attention. ICH governance is largely local and national, predicated on many of the forms of globalization that we have traced through this book: folk and vernacular traditions have value in and of themselves; nations should turn to culture and the arts to nurture their distinctiveness; because it belongs to everyone, music must benefit from support that recognizes how it matters locally and globally.

The new 21st-century forms of action and agency have also been particularly influential in the emergence of applied and engaged ethnomusicology. Applied ethnomusicologists turn to the lived-in world as the field in which they conduct research and mobilize music to bring about tangible change. As a discipline and field, applied ethnomusicology has developed along the borders shared with various academic and social organizations. There is recognition that action and intervention must be implemented locally in order to respond to real-life problems and crises. Above all, the intangible must be approached in order to produce tangible solutions. Increasingly, ethnomusicology is undergoing a sweeping disciplinary transition that enhances its commitment to the collective, the coequal presence of musicians and scholars in the field. Such commitment has also been significant because it reconnects the local to the global, realizing an epistemological sea change necessitating the recognition that world music matters.

Music matters in a changing world

As I reach the final section in this book, I reflect both on the past and future of world music, indeed, on the ways in which music will increasingly matter in a changing world. There are many pressing questions that accompany my reflections in this closing section, but perhaps none more so than, What will survive of the world music of the past at the present rate of precipitous change? The difficulty of sustaining music's materiality in Dadpur—and the very fragility of life, human and beyond in the natural world—will no longer be a factor of its remoteness, but rather it will be connected to an Anthropocene whose survival is ever more tenuous.

It has been a premise of this book that the ways in which music matters in the world have multiplied and expanded as history becomes increasingly global. Basic issues and questions remain intact throughout history, but they spread globally with growing intensity. Diaspora, though it first described the spread of Greek communities to the Aegean and Asia Minor in Antiquity, and then developed specific historical meaning with the Jewish diaspora at the beginning of the Common Era, is now a global condition of many cultures and religions. Nationalism, a powerful motivation for emerging nations worldwide in the 19th century and a source of musical symbols as empire collapsed in the 20th century, has as many negative as positive forms in the 21st century. Some folk practices remain intimate and local, while others flood the stages of international festivals and transnational refugee movements.

The globalization that world music accompanies and articulates does not diminish with the passage of time, but rather accelerates, subject to escalating change, often turbulent and contested, and consistently leaving its impact on world music. New and different names accrue to the changing forms of globalization. We may hesitate to speak about universal properties of music, but we recognize related phenomena when tracing the mobility of music across transnational networks. If we refrain from claiming that all people have folk song, there is widespread belief that individuals, like linguistic or religious communities, and nations, possess musical practices that express their personal identities. Where do these new forms of globalization lie, and how might we recognize them? In what remains I turn to three areas in which it has become fruitful to search for the materiality that makes world music matter in the world inescapably shaped by globalization.

Global Indigeneity. In the long history of global encounter Indigenous peoples and music all-too-frequently appeared on the peripheries of the world, where their musical practices were marginalized in various ways (see Chapter 1). In the 21st century, however, there is growing recognition that Indigenous peoples are present throughout the world. It has become necessary to rewrite national and transnational histories to include Indigenous narratives that have been erased, often the most brutal forms of oppression and exclusion. Retrieving Indigenous music as world music is now critical because of the ontological paradigm shifts that quickly follow, not least among them the ineluctable presence of the environment and the natural world in global Indigenous musical thought.

The natural world and posthuman musical aesthetics. The expanded search for music's materialities has both deployed and dismantled the borders between human and natural worlds, yielding a musical aesthetics that transcends the limitations of human experience. That aesthetics is often explicit in global Indigeneity, for example, a recognition that animals make music that expresses alternative ways of living in the natural world. We witness this in Indigenous understandings of composition, which often take place in domains beyond human experience. Healing practices, for example, those of shamans, mobilize spirits, often animals, to engage with the human body. A musical aesthetics immanent in the natural world also coincides with the scientific studies of posthumanism. Why, many music scholars increasingly claim, should there be a separation between culture and nature? The answers to this question once again make music matter, for they lead specifically to recognition that humans are not the sole occupants of the Anthropocene.

Cultural sustainability/musical survival. The mobility and materiality of music have long generated fears about the fragility of music in cultures whose existence was externally threatened. Such fears, especially when directed toward world music, are greater in the 21st century than ever before. Entire cultures and the music they sustain face natural disaster. The spectre of coastal erosion along the Gulf Coast of the southern United States could soon lead to the disappearance of the historically rich music cultures of Cajuns and Isleños in Louisiana, with their French- and Spanish-language traditions stretching centuries into the past. In the face of climate change, cultural sustainability emerges as one more condition of world music.

World music matters more than ever before. It does so because the instrument builders in Dadpur enter an even more complex global network as they transform the material world around them into music that ensures their survival. It does so because immigrants and refugees gain dignity by holding on to the music that gives them a new life in a threatening world. It does so because the musical thought and practices that world musicians bear with them continue to encompass more rather than less in a vast, changing world.

References

Chapter 1: In the beginning . . . Myth and meaning in world music

David W. Ames and Anthony V. King, *Glossary of Hausa Music and Its Social Contexts* (Northwestern University Press, 1971)

Pi-yen Chen (ed.), *Chinese Buddhist Monastic Chants* (A-R Editions, 2010) (CD included)

Jean de Léry, *History of a Voyage to the Land of Brazil, Otherwise Called America*, trans. Janet Whatley (University of California Press, 1999)

A. J. Racy, *Making Music in the Arab World: The Culture and Artistry of ṭarab* (Cambridge University Press, 2003)

The Rig Veda: An Anthology, trans. and annotated by Wendy Doniger O'Flaherty (Penguin, 1981)

Charles Seeger, *Studies in Musicology, 1935–1975* (University of California Press, 1977)

Chapter 2: The West and the world

Roger D. Abrahams and John F. Szwed (eds), *After Africa: Extracts from British Travel Accounts and Journals of the Seventeenth, Eighteenth, and Nineteenth Centuries Concerning the Slaves, Their Manners, and Customs in the British West Indies* (Yale University Press, 1983)

Michael Denning, *Noise Uprising: The Audiopolitics of a World Musical Revolution* (Verso, 2015)

Emmanuel Chukwudi Eze (ed.), *Race and the Enlightenment: A Reader* (Blackwell, 1997)

Johann Gottfried Herder, *Journal meiner Reise im Jahr 1769* (Reclam, 1976)
Johann Gottfried Herder, *Volkslieder*, 2 vols (Weygandsche Buchhandlung, 1778–9)
Friedrich A. Kittler, *Discourse Networks, 1800/1900*, trans. Michael Metzer (Stanford University Press, 1990)
Robert Lachmann, *The Oriental Music Broadcasts, 1936–1937: A Musical Ethnography of Mandatory Palestine*, ed. Ruth F. Davis (A-R Editions, 2013)

Chapter 3: Between myth and history

Congress of Cairo, *Recueil des travaux du Congrès de Musique Arabe* (Imprimerie nationale, Boulac, 1934)
Virginia Danielson, *The Voice of Egypt: Umm Kulthum, Arabic Song, and Egyptian Society in the Twentieth Century* (University of Chicago Press, 1997)
Ibn Khaldun, *The Muqaddimah: An Introduction to History*, trans. Franz Rosenthal, 3 vols (Pantheon, 1958)
Richard C. Jankowsky, *Stambeli: Music, Trance, and Alterity in Tunisia* (University of Chicago Press, 2010)
Robert Lachmann, *Jewish Cantillation and Song in the Isle of Djerba* (Archives of Oriental Music, The Hebrew University, 1940)
Albert B. Lord, *The Singer of Tales* (Harvard University Press, 1960)
A. J. Racy, 'Comparative Musicologists in the Field: Reflections on the Cairo Congress of Arab Music, 1932', in *This Thing Called Music: Essays in Honor of Bruno Nettl*, ed. Victoria Lindsay Levine and Philip V. Bohlman (Rowman & Littlefield, 2015), 137–50
Edward Said, *Orientalism* (Random House, 1978)
Guillaume-André Villoteau, 'De l'état actuel de l'art musical en Egypte', in *Description de l'Egypte*, 2nd edn (C. L. F. Panckoucke, 1826)

Chapter 4: Music of the folk

L. Achim von Arnim and Clemens Brentano, *Des Knaben Wunderhorn: Alte deutsche Lieder* (Mohr und Zimmer, 1806 and 1808)
Moses Asch and Alan Lomax (eds), *The Leadbelly Songbook: The Ballads, Blues and Folksongs of Huddie Ledbetter* (Oak Publications, 1962)
Philip V. Bohlman and Otto Holzapfel, *The Folk Songs of Ashkenaz* (A-R Editions, 2001)

S. M. Ginsburg and P. S. Marek, *Evreiskie narodnye pesni v Rossii* [Jewish Folk Songs from Russia] (Voskhod, 1901)
Lars-Christian Koch, *My Heart Sings: Die Lieder Rabindranath Tagores zwischen Tradition und Moderne* (LIT 2012)
Rabindranath Tagore, *Gitabitan* (Visva-Bharati, 1966)

Chapter 5: Music of the nations

Benedict Anderson, *Imagined Communities: Reflections on the Origins and Spread of Nationalism*, revised edn (Verso, 2006)
Dorothea Baumann and Dinko Fabris (eds), *The History of the IMS (1927–2017)* (Bärenreiter, 2017)
Johann Gottfried Herder and Philip V. Bohlman, *Song Loves the Masses: Herder on Music and Nationalism* (University of California Press, 2017)
Grove Music Online. <http://www.oxfordmusiconline.com/>
Michael Herzfeld, *Cultural Intimacy: Social Poetics in the Nation-State* (Routledge, 1997)
John Philip Sousa, *National, Patriotic and Typical Airs of All Lands* (H. Coleman, 1890)
Dafni Tragaki (ed.), *Empire of Song: Europe and Nation in the Eurovision Song Contest* (Scarecrow, 2013)

Chapter 6: Diaspora

Amit Chaudhuri, *Afternoon Raag* (William Heinemann, 1993)
W. E. B. Du Bois, *The Souls of Black Folk*, ed. Henry Louis Gates, Jr (Bantam, 1989)
Janet Topp Fargion, Taarab *Music in Zanzibar in the Twentieth Century: A Story of 'Old Is Gold' and Flying Spirits* (Ashgate, 2014)
Paul Gilroy, *The Black Atlantic: Double Consciousness and Modernity* (Harvard University Press, 1993)
A. Z. Idelsohn, *Hebräisch-orientalischer Melodienschatz*, 10 vols (Benjamin Harz et al., 1914–32)
Ashish Rajadhyaksha, *Indian Cinema: A Very Short Introduction* (Oxford University Press, 2016)
Timothy Rommen, 'Landscapes of Diaspora', in Philip V. Bohlman (ed.), *The Cambridge History of World Music*, 557–83 (Cambridge University Press, 2013)

Chapter 7: Empire, decoloniality, and the globalization of world music

Walter Benjamin, *The Arcades Project*, trans. Howard Eiland and Kevin McLaughlin (Harvard University Press, 1999)

Simon Broughton, Mark Ellingham, and Richard Trillo, *World Music*, vol. 1: *Africa, Europe and the Middle East* (The Rough Guides, 1999)

Simon Broughton and Mark Ellingham (eds), *World Music*, vol. 2: *Latin and North America, Caribbean, India, Asia and Pacific* (The Rough Guides, 2000)

Sebastian Klotz, Philip V. Bohlman, and Lars-Christian Koch (eds), *Sounding Cities: Auditory Transformations in Berlin, Chicago, and Kolkata* (LIT Verlag, 2018)

Carl Stumpf, *The Origins of Music*, ed. and trans. David Trippett (Oxford University Press, 2012)

Chapter 8: World music matters

Baul Songs: <https://ich.unesco.org/en/RL/baul-songs-00107>

Bharata-Muni, *The Nāṭyaśāstra*, 2 vols, trans. Manomohan Ghosh (The Asiatic Society, 1961)

Steven Feld, *Jazz Cosmopolitanism in Accra: Five Musical Years in Ghana* (Duke University Press, 2012)

Johann Gottfried Herder and Philip V. Bohlman, *Song Loves the Masses: Herder on Music and Nationalism* (University of California Press, 2017)

Ana María Ochoa Gautier, *Aurality: Listening and Knowledge in Nineteenth-Century Colombia* (Duke University Press, 2014)

UNESCO, *Intangible Cultural Heritage* <https://ich.unesco.org/>

Further reading

The following suggestions are intended as a starting point for the reader wishing to explore further the themes discussed in each of the chapters of this book.

Chapter 1: In the beginning... Myth and meaning in world music

Marc Benamou, *Rasa: Affect and Interaction in Javanese Musical Aesthetics* (Oxford University Press, 2010)

Regula Burckhardt Qureshi, *Sufi Music of India and Pakistan: Sound, Context and Meaning in Qawwali* (University of Chicago Press, 1995) (CD included)

Nicholas Cook and Mark Everist (eds), *Rethinking Music* (Oxford University Press, 1999)

Jeffers Engelhardt and Philip V. Bohlman (eds), *Resounding Transcendence: Transitions in Music, Religion, and Ritual* (Oxford University Press, 2016)

Lewis Rowell, *Music and Musical Thought in Early India* (University of Chicago Press, 1992)

Gary Tomlinson, *A Million Years of Music: The Emergence of Human Modernity* (Zone Books, 2015)

Nils L. Wallin, Björn Merker, and Steven Brown (eds), *The Origins of Music* (MIT Press, 2000)

Chapter 2: The West and the world

Georgina Born and Dave Hesmondhalgh (eds), *Western Music and Its Others: Difference, Representation, and Appropriation in Music* (University of California Press, 2000)

Erika Brady, *A Spiral Way: How the Phonograph Changed Ethnography* (University Press of Mississippi, 1999)

Emmanuel Chukwudi Eze (ed.), *Race and the Enlightenment: A Reader* (Blackwell, 1997)

Klaus P. Wachsmann et al. (eds and trans.), *Hornbostel Opera Omnia* (Martinus Nijhoff, 1975)

Chapter 3: Between myth and history

Philip V. Bohlman and Nada Petković (eds), *Balkan Epic: Song, History, Modernity* (Scarecrow, 2012)

Jonathan Glasser, *The Lost Paradise: Andalusi Music in Urban North Africa* (University of Chicago Press, 2016)

Israel J. Katz, *Henry George Farmer and the First International Congress of Arab Music (Cairo 1932)* (Brill, 2015)

Kristina Nelson, *The Art of Reciting the Qur'an* (University of Texas Press, 1985)

Chapter 4: Music of the folk

Béla Bartók, *Hungarian Folk Music*, trans. M. C. Calvacoressi (Oxford University Press, 1931)

Malcolm Chapman, *The Celts: The Construction of a Myth* (Macmillan, 1992)

Victor Greene, *A Passion for Polka: Old-Time Music in America* (University of California Press, 1992)

Alan Lomax, *Hard Hitting Songs for Hard-Hit People* (Oak Publications, 1967)

John A. Lomax and Alan Lomax, *Folk Song: U.S.A., the 111 Best American Ballads*, ed. Charles Seeger and Ruth Crawford Seeger (Duell, Sloan and Pearce, 1947)

Mark Slobin, *Folk Music: A Very Short Introduction* (Oxford University Press, 2011)

Chapter 5: Music of the nations

Philip V. Bohlman, *Music, Nationalism, and the Making of the New Europe*, 2nd edn (Routledge, 2011)

R. K. Prahbu (ed.), *Songs of Freedom: An Anthology of National and International Songs from Various Countries of the World* (Popular Prakashan, 1967)

Ivan Raykoff and Robert Deam Tobin (eds), *A Song for Europe: Popular Music and Politics in the Eurovision Song Contest* (Ashgate, 2007)

Chapter 6: Diaspora

Sidney J. Lemelle and Robin D. G. Kelley, *Imagining Home: Class, Culture, and Nationalism in the African Diaspora* (Verso, 1994)

Peter Manuel, *Cassette Culture: Popular Music and Culture in North India* (University of Chicago Press, 1993)

Helen Myers, *Music of Hindu Trinidad: Songs from the India Diaspora* (University of Chicago Press, 1998)

Carol E. Robertson (ed.), *Musical Repercussions of 1492: Encounters in Text and Performance* (Smithsonian Institution Press, 1992)

Chapter 7: Empire, decoloniality, and the globalization of world music

Stanley Appelbaum, *The Chicago World's Fair of 1893: A Photographic Record* (Dover, 1980)

Daphne Berdahl, Matti Bunzl, and Martha Lampland (eds), *Altering States: Ethnographies of Transition in Eastern Europe and the Former Soviet Union* (University of Michigan Press, 2000)

Ronald Radano and Tejumola Olaniyan (eds), *Audible Empire: Music, Global Politics, Critique* (Duke University Press, 2016)

Mark Slobin (ed.), *Retuning Culture: Musical Change in Central and Eastern Europe* (Duke University Press, 1996)

Chapter 8: World music matters

Charles Capwell, *Sailing on the Sea of Love: The Music of the Bauls of Bengal* (Seagull, 2010)

Alex E. Chávez, *Sounds of Crossing: Music, Migration, and the Aural Poetics of Huapango Arribeño* (Duke University Press, 2017)
Bernd Clausen, Ursula Hemetek, Eva Sæther, and European Music Council (eds), *Music in Motion: Diversity and Dialogue in Europe* (Transcript, 2009)
Erle C. Ellis, *Anthropocene: A Very Short Introduction* (Oxford University Press, 2018)
Holly Watkins, *Musical Vitalities: Ventures in a Biotic Aesthetics of Music* (University of Chicago Press, 2018)

Listening

With each revolution in digital technology over the course of the past four decades the access to audio and video recordings of world music has expanded exponentially. Archival documentation of early recordings and the ethnographic collections of research and educational institutions worldwide are now available through internet links. Commercial recordings circulate globally, accessible on internet platforms such as YouTube or through 'cloud' storage such as Spotify. Recordings that employ earlier forms of technology, however, have not disappeared, and they frequently serve as signposts during the moments of sea change in the modern history of world music. Several of these recordings, especially anthologies, have been selected and listed below to give the reader a feel for the artists and genres of music described in each chapter of this book.

Chapter 1: In the beginning...Myth and meaning in world music

Hesperus, *Spain in the New World: Renaissance, Baroque and Native American Music from New Spain*, Golden Apple GACD 7552 (1990)

Jean Jenkins and Poul Rovsing Olsen (eds), *Music in the World of Islam*, 6 LPs, Tangent TBX 601 (1976)

Various artists, *The Best of Amir Khusrau*, 2 CDs, Music Today (2004)

Chapter 2: The West and the world

Chieftains, *Santiago*, RCA/BMG 09026-68602-2 (1996)

Erich Moritz von Hornbostel (comp.), *The Demonstration Collection of E. M. von Hornbostel and the Berlin Phonogramm-Archiv*, with commentaries by Kurt Reinhard and George List, 2 LPs and accompanying booklet, Ethnic Folkways FE 4175 (1963)

Erich Moritz von Hornbostel (comp.), *Music of the Orient*, 2 LPs and accompanying booklet, Ethnic Folkways FE 4157 (1979, orig. 1934)

Music! The Berlin Phonogramm-Archiv 1900–2011 in 111 Recordings, 5 CDs, Ethnologisches Museum, Staatliche Museen zu Berlin (2011)

Chapter 3: Between myth and history

Congrès du Caire, 1932, 2 CDs, Archives Sonores de la Phonothèque Nationale, APN 88/9–10

Umm Kulthūm's recordings are widely available on EMI Egypt, increasingly on remastered CDs, and on the internet.

Chapter 4: Music of the folk

The Celtic Heartbeat Collection, Celtic Heartbeat 82732 (1995)

Leadbelly, *Leadbelly Sings Folk Songs*, Folkways FA2488

Alan Lomax (ed.), *World Library of Folk and Primitive Music: The Historic Series*, projected 40 vols, Rounder Records

Muzsikás, *The Bartók Album*, Hannibal HNCD 1439 (1999)

Polish-American Dance Music—The Early Recordings: 1927–33, Folklyric Records 9026

Harry Smith (ed.), *Anthology of American Folk Music*, 6 CDs, Smithsonian Folkways 40090/A 28746-A 28751 (1997)

Richard K. Spottswood (ed.), *Folk Music in America*, 15 vols, Library of Congress LBC 1–15

Chapter 5: Music of the nations

Songs from the Eurovision Song Contest, live performances, as well as official and unofficial videos, are widely available on the internet website, <https://eurovision.tv/>.

Chapter 6: Diaspora

Gerda Lechleitner (ed.), *The Collection of Abraham Zvi Idelsohn (1911–1913)* (Verlag der Österreichischen Akademie der Wissenschaften, 2005)

The most comprehensive collection of Bob Marley's recordings is: Bob Marley & the Wailers, *Songs of Freedom*, 4-CD set (Island Records, 1992)

Chapter 7: Empire, decoloniality, and the globalization of world music

Rough Guides: A Guide to the Rough Guide Music Series, RGNET 902 CD (2001)

The Rough Guide to Salsa, RGNET 1184 CD (2007)

The Rough Guide to Salsa Dance, RGNET 1156 CD (2005)

World Music Festival: Chicago 2000, 'Big Chicago Records' BCR 008 (2000)

Chapter 8: World music matters

Purna Chandra Das Baul, *The Bengal Minstrel*, Nonesuch H-72068 (1975)

Zaide, eine Flucht, <https://www.youtube.com/watch?v=8xPPndgffRs>; accessed on 22 July 2019

Index

A

B

C

F

G

H

I

J

K

L

M

N

O

P

S

AFRICAN HISTORY

A Very Short Introduction

John Parker & Richard Rathbone

Essential reading for anyone interested in the African continent and the diversity of human history, this *Very Short Introduction* looks at Africa's past and reflects on the changing ways it has been imagined and represented. Key themes in current thinking about Africa's history are illustrated with a range of fascinating historical examples, drawn from over 5 millennia across this vast continent.

> 'A very well informed and sharply stated historiography . . . should be in every historiography student's kitbag. A tour de force . . . it made me think a great deal.'
>
> Terence Ranger,
> **The Bulletin of the School of Oriental and African Studies**

EARLY MUSIC

A Very Short Introduction

Thomas Forrest Kelly

The music of the medieval, Renaissance, and baroque periods have been repeatedly discarded and rediscovered ever since they were new. In recent years interest in music of the past has taken on particular meaning, representing two specific trends: first, a rediscovery of little-known underappreciated repertories, and second, an effort to recover lost performing styles. In this VSI, Thomas Forrest Kelly frames chapters on the forms, techniques, and repertories of the medieval, Renaissance, and baroque periods with discussion of why old music has been and should be revived, along with a short history of early music revivals.

www.oup.com/vsi

Film Music

A Very Short Introduction

Kathryn Kalinak

This *Very Short Introduction* provides a lucid, accessible, and engaging overview of the subject of film music. Beginning with an analysis of the music from a well-known sequence in the film Reservoir Dogs, the book focuses on the most central issues in the practice of film music. Expert author Kay Kalinak takes readers behind the scenes to understand both the practical aspects of film music - what it is and how it is composed - and also the theories that have been developed to explain why film musicworks. This compact book not entertains with the fascinating stories of the composers and performers who have shaped film music across the globe but also gives readers a broad sense for the key questions in film music studies today.

> 'Kathryn Kalinak has emerged as one of the freshest and most authoritative commentatory on film music of her generation.'
>
> **Michael Quinn, Classical Music**

www.oup.com/vsi

Folk Music

A Very Short Introduction

Mark Slobin

This stimulating *Very Short Introduction* throws open the doors on a remarkably diverse musical genre, with a world-wide reach that goes far beyond America's shores to discuss folk music of every possible kind and in every corner of the globe. Written by award-winning ethnomusicologist Mark Slobin this is the first compact introduction to folk music that offers a truly global perspective. Slobin offers an extraordinarily generous portrait of folk music, one that embraces a Russian wedding near the Arctic Circle, a group song in a small rainforest village in Brazil, and an Uzbek dance tune in Afghanistan. He looks in detail at three poignant songs from three widely separated regions--northern Afghanistan, Jewish Eastern Europe, and the Anglo-American world--with musical notation and lyrics included. He goes on to sketch out the turbulent times of folk music today and tomorrow, confronting new possibilities, frameworks, and challenges.

THE BLUES

A Very Short Introduction

Elijah Wald

This VSI provides a brief history of the blues genre's main movements and most influential artists and gives a sense of the breadth of the blues field. Beginning with the music's roots in African and African-American styles, European folk music, and popular forms such as minstrelsy and ragtime, it traces how blues evolved over the course of the twentieth century as both a discrete genre and a basic ingredient in virtually all American pop styles from jazz to hip-hop.

www.oup.com/vsi

Spanish Literature

A Very Short Introduction

Jo Labanyi

This *Very Short Introduction* explores the rich literary history of Spanish literature, which resonates with contemporary debates on transnationalism and cultural diversity. The book introduces a general readership to the ways in which Spanish literature has been read, in and outside Spain, explaining misconceptions, outlining the insights of recent scholarship and suggesting new readings. It highlights the precocious modernity of much early modern Spanish literature, and shows how the gap between modern ideas and social reality stimulated creative literary responses in subsequent periods; as well as how contemporary writers have adjusted to Spain's recent accelerated modernization.

International Migration

A Very Short Introduction

Khalid Koser

Why has international migration become an issue of such intense public and political concern? How closely linked are migrants with terrorist organizations? What factors lie behind the dramatic increase in the number of women migrating? This *Very Short Introduction* examines the phenomenon of international human migration - both legal and illegal. Taking a global look at politics, economics, and globalization, the author presents the human side of topics such as asylum and refugees, human trafficking, migrant smuggling, development, and the international labour force.

www.oup.com/vsi